FOOD PROCESSOR COOKING IS SWEEPING THE COUNTRY:

"The most important invention since the first electric mixer." —*Julia Child*

"For anyone who does a great deal of cooking, it's as necessary as a good stove." —*James Beard*

"The food processor is the greatest thing to happen to the well-equipped American kitchen since refrigeration." —*Craig Claiborne*

A MOSTLY FRENCH FOOD PROCESSOR COOKBOOK

Your guide to a new world of faster French cooking.

COLETTE ROSSANT, the French-born author of *Cooking with Colette* and translator of *Paul Bocuse's French Cooking*, lives in Manhattan with her husband and four children. Mme. Rossant first became interested in cooking when she was a child in Paris and was inspired by the family cook, a Cordon Bleu chef. She teaches French cooking in her townhouse, is chairman of the language department at a nearby private school, and gardens for pleasure.

JILL HARRIS HERMAN, a writer and editor who enjoys fine cooking, spent the past ten years in Manhattan and now resides with her husband and daughter in Dallas, Texas. Ms. Herman attended Wells College, graduated from the University of Pennsylvania, and is a former member of the editorial staff of *The New Yorker* magazine.

A MOSTLY FRENCH
FOOD PROCESSOR
COOKBOOK

by

Colette Rossant
and Jill Harris Herman

ILLUSTRATED BY JAMES ROSSANT

A PLUME BOOK
NEW AMERICAN LIBRARY
TIMES MIRROR
NEW YORK, LONDON, AND SCARBOROUGH, ONTARIO

PLUME TRADEMARK REG. U.S. PAT. OFF. AND FOREIGN COUNTRIES
REGISTERED TRADEMARK—MARCA REGISTRADA
HECHO EN FORGE VILLAGE, MASS., U.S.A.

SIGNET, SIGNET CLASSICS, MENTOR, PLUME and
MERIDIAN BOOKS are published in the United States by
The New American Library, Inc.,
1301 Avenue of the Americas, New York, New York 10019,
in Canada by The New American Library of Canada Limited,
81 Mack Avenue, Scarborough, Ontario MIL 1M8,
in the United Kingdom by The New English Library Limited,
Barnard's Inn, Holborn, London, E.C. 1, England.

First Plume Printing, October, 1977

3 4 5 6 7 8 9 10 11

PRINTED IN THE UNITED STATES OF AMERICA

To Cécile and Margaret

Contents

Introduction

We offer here an assortment of dishes, mostly French, all quite colorful, that range from the simple yet distinctive to the truly elegant. Almost all share one thing: were it not for the food processor, we would not attempt them, save for very special occasions.

We haven't included recipes that call for little more than the chopping of a single onion or the grating of a small piece of Parmesan, but have chosen only those—a fresh tomato and basil soup, a pungent rillette, a lobster soufflé in crepe with a Sauce Coulis—that will set your food processor singing.

We have sought to fill this book with dishes that are a bit out of the ordinary, recipes rarely found elsewhere, to compose a cookbook that will stand on its own. To be sure, many of the sauces and doughs are classics, though their methods of preparation are not. But, when selecting a hearty beef stew, we chose a brisket with cranberries and green peppercorns over a tried-and-true beef bourgignon. After all, once you have mastered your kitchen machine, adapting old stand-bys will be easy.

Colette Rossant, who spent much of her childhood in France in the company of good cooks and gastronomes, devised the recipes and tested them on the many food processors that line her kitchen counters. I drove back and forth between my apartment on Manhattan's Upper West Side and her townhouse in SoHo, at the far end of the city, to taste every dish before we wrote it up. Eager to learn the rationale behind techniques that are as natural to Colette as breathing, I bombarded her with questions; the result is a fortuitous one. Though many of the entries will challenge the ablest chef, the directions should be so clear that a competent, enthusiastic cook can be all but assured of success when, for the first time, he wraps a whole bluefish stuffed with shrimp in pastry dough. Throughout, we offer advice on how to use your food processor, what it can do, and what it cannot.

The food processor is a tool that takes some getting used to. Before trying any recipes, we advise you to read all the manuals that pertain to your kitchen machine as well as our summary of it. Next, look over the list of special instructions at the beginning of this book and refer to it as needed; much is common-sense advice that will help make using your food processor easier. If you are new to your machine, set it in a convenient spot and practice with a plentiful supply of apples, onions, carrots, bread, cabbage, cheese, whatever, until you feel at ease. Then, begin!

Jill Harris Herman

Special Instructions for Food Processors with Work Bowls

Almost all processing, except for the slicing and shredding of vegetables, is done in the work bowl by the steel blade.

When chopping with the steel blade:

1. Ingredients should be of fairly equal size.
2. Meat, fish, and soft vegetables should be processed in small batches, not more than a cup or two at a time.
3. It is not necessary to remove tendons from meat before chopping.

4. It is not necessary to remove stems from parsley, dill, or even spinach, unless you are using it for garnish.

5. Ingredients need not be of the same consistency to be chopped together, provided you start with the hardest, such as carrots, and add the softer ingredients, such as onions, after a few seconds. Process just until all ingredients are evenly chopped.

6. With soft ingredients, such as mushrooms or onions, it is best to keep turning the work bowl on and off, if only to gauge yourself. When necessary, stop the machine and scrape the sides with a rubber spatula.

7. If overblending is a persistent problem (and it usually is a problem at first), watch carefully, turn the work bowl on and off frequently, and stop the machine from time to time to check on consistency. If you stop frequently enough, even meat should retain its texture.

8. Do not throw out your disasters: onion juices can be added to soups and sauces; liquefied meats and mushrooms to gravies and stews.

9. Parsley, onions, bread crumbs, grated cheese, and other frequently used ingredients can be processed in quantity, sealed, and stored in the refrigerator (see page 25).

10. To chop ice, Parmesan cheese, or other hard substances, start the machine and drop the ingredients, piece by piece, through the feed tube; in time, the consistency will be just right. Bread crumbs can also be processed this way or in a large batch all at once.

To grate hard cheeses, such as Parmesan, with the Cuisinart or Farberware, use the steel blade, *not* the grating blade—it is not strong enough. With the Robot Coupe, either the grating blade or steel blade can be used.

Never add more than two cups of liquid to the work bowl; it will leak out the bottom.

To puree soups with the steel blade, add the solids to the work bowl first. With the machine running, pour in two cups of liquid at most. Remove the mixture to a bowl or saucepan and add the remaining liquids; mix well with a wooden spoon.

When using the steel blade, do not add pepper or other dry spices; they stick to the bottom. Season afterwards.

When making egg-based sauces, it is usually necessary to start with two yolks, and with three in the Robot Coupe. Mix the eggs with the steel or plastic blade until they are a bit frothy, then slowly add a few drops of liquid. Pause for several seconds before adding more liquid in a slow steady stream.

If sauces curdle or separate, place in the work bowl and beat with the steel blade or plastic blade until they re-emulsify.

For most doughs, all ingredients can be added at once and mixed with the steel or plastic blade. If a pâte brisée or other butter dough begins to crumble, add a tablespoon or two of flour.

When making dough, for best results, do not wait for it to form a ball. Instead, when the dough detaches from the sides of the bowl and begins to cling together, stop the machine and roll the dough yourself.

To make a *beurre manié* in the work bowl, add two tablespoons of butter and flour, and mix with your plastic or steel blade.

To make chiffonades of leafy vegetables with the shredding blade, do not fill up the feed tube. Add only a few leaves and, when the machine is running, press with the pusher.

Please follow all safety precautions:

1. *Always wait for blades to stop before removing cover or splash guard from work bowl.*
2. *Be very careful with the steel blade; it is sharp!*
3. *Always hold the steel blade in place or remove it before pouring.*
4. *Never push vegetables in the feed tube with your fingers; always use the pusher.*
5. *Keep all blades out of the reach of children.*

Special Instructions for Food Processors with Specific Attachments

Set up the food processor with the blender or most frequently used attachment in place. Store attachments used often nearby.

Set out all equipment needed at the start of each dish. In this book, attachments to be used will be listed at the top of each recipe.

Use the settings recommended in your instruction manual. In general, unless an ingredient is fragile, the speed used depends on how fast you want to go and how much control is required. For example, when chopping or slicing a carrot, you can go as fast as you please, but when preparing juliennes, go slowly so the strands will be long and will not break.

1. For shredding and slicing most vegetables, medium speed seems best.
2. When grinding meat or fish in the meat grinder, use the high or medium speed.
3. When whipping cream or beating ingredients that might splatter, always start with the lowest speed and work up to that which will give you the consistency you want.

When chopping with the blender:

1. Process small quantities, not more than a cup or so at a time.
2. Stop often to lift the ingredients at the bottom up and over the blades with a rubber spatula.
3. When chopping mushrooms, onions, and other very soft ingredients, use the manual control. Stop often to lift with a rubber spatula and to check on consistency.
4. So that watery vegetables, such as spinach, avocados, and potatoes, tumble freely instead of lodging at the bottom, add a tablespoon of liquid to the blender.

5. To mince parsley, stems and all, cut the stems first; chop in small batches at low speed, stopping frequently to lift ingredients with a rubber spatula.

Other uses for the blender:

To puree vegetables, always add one-quarter cup of milk, cream, or cooking liquid to the blender.

Only process two or three cups of liquid at a time, unless your blender can be filled to the top without splattering.

To puree soups, never add more solids than liquid. For best results, puree soups in at least two batches.

To blend egg-based sauces, start with one or two egg yolks and mix until frothy. Pour the liquid, in a slow steady stream, through the opening in the blender lid or "feed tube." When the sauce has begun to thicken and a cup of liquid has been added, stop the blender and turn the sauce at the bottom up and over the blades with a rubber spatula so that it does not get too stiff.

If sauces curdle or separate, set your blender on low speed and slowly pour in the sauce; continue until the sauce re-emulsifies.

To make a *beurre manié*, add a tablespoon of flour and a tablespoon of butter and beat until it forms a paste.

Cooked or leftover meat and fish can be ground in the meat grinder or chopped, in small batches, in the blender. When using the blender, if the meat is very dry, moisten it with two or three tablespoons of broth or other liquid.

Pepper and other dry spices can be added to the blender, if desired; to mix in, turn the manual control.

Grate bread crumbs with the grating blade unless the blender is already in place.

Hard cheeses and nuts can be grated by the grating blade, the coffee grinder attachment, or the blender. For expediency's sake, we usually choose the attachment that is already in place, but the choice is yours.

Parsley, onions, grated cheese, and bread crumbs can be processed in large batches, then sealed and stored in the refrigerator.

Since vegetable slicer/shredders vary with each machine, please follow your instruction manual. These safety rules are standard:

1. *Always guide vegetables in the feed tube with the pusher, never your fingers.*
2. *Always wait for the motor to stop before opening the cover.*

Read the instruction manual carefully for suggestions on the uses, maintenance, setting up, and cleaning of your food processor. Please follow all safety precautions, including these:

1. *Turn the motor off before changing attachments.*
2. *Watch out for attachment units that are not in use.*
3. *Keep all blades out of the reach of children.*
4. *Be very careful with sharp blades.*

Food Processors: An Evaluation

The food processor falls into that rare category of necessary luxuries we had never suspected were missing from our lives; now, in all likelihood, we will never again be without one. A skilled apprentice and sauce maker, the food processor inspires us to cook well at almost every turn, to prepare dishes we would not otherwise undertake, and to cook elaborately more frequently. Yet a food processor is simply a kitchen machine with a single motor base that, when fully equipped or added to, can do the following: chop, puree, julienne, and slice vegetables; grate cheeses and bread crumbs; blend sauces and spreads; grind meats and fish; knead bread and pastry doughs; and, in many cases, beat and fold eggs and cream. In order to enjoy the full range of possibilities, from making your own pâtés to whipping up light and lovely soufflés, it is often necessary to go beyond the basic food processor purchase to acquire the one item that is missing and needed—usually either a meat grinder attachment or a portable electric beater—which will enable your kitchen machine to perform all food processor functions.

Of the more than a dozen food processors on the market at this time, we judge eight to be exceptionally fine. These are the Bosch, Braun, Cuisinart, Farberware, Kitchen Aid K5-A, Oster Kitchen Center, Robot Coupe, and Starmix. Though they range in price from one hundred twenty dollars to close to five hundred, they are all variations on one of two themes: those that require many separate, specific attachments* and those in which almost all work is done in a single work bowl by a flat steel blade.† In general, the first group offers near-perfect results; the second, the convenience of a machine that is always at the ready and easy to clean.

Below, we offer our evaluation and comparison of each of these kitchen machines. Among the qualities we consider are performance, ease of use, ease of cleaning, size, relative cost, sturdiness, appearance, and the extra equipment needed. If you are thinking of buying a machine, we hope these summaries will help you choose a food processor that makes sense for you, based on your cooking likes and needs, the size of your household, the size of your kitchen, your finances, the equipment you already have on hand, and whether you lean toward convenience or perfection. If you already own a food processor, the summary provides information that is specific to the use and care of your machine.

Bosch Magic Mixer,™ Deluxe

Motor base with two attachment units
Plastic blender, lid with feed tube, funnel
5½-quart stainless-steel mixing bowl with splash guard

- 2 rotary whisks
- three-pronged dough hook/folding attachment

Vegetable slicing/shredding attachment with round feed tube and pusher

- plastic bowl with cover
- 4 blades for slicing/shredding 5 ways

(2 speeds plus manual)

* Bosch, Braun, Kitchen Aid K5-A, Oster Kitchen Center, Starmix.
† Cuisinart, Farberware, Robot Coupe.

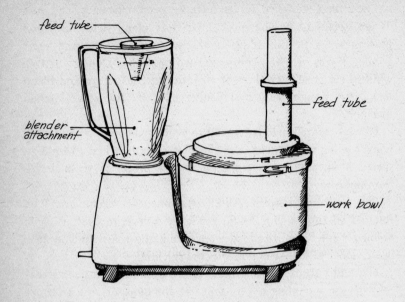

feed tube

blender
attachment

feed tube

work bowl

Accessories:

Meat grinder with the following attachments:

- biscuit piper
- cheese grater
- fruit press
- pasta maker
- sausage stuffer

Extrusion vegetable shredder with chute for continuous flow,
    4 blades
Bean chipper
Coffee grinder
Hand beater/mixer attachment
Ice cream freezer
Juicer
Potato peeler
Potato shredding blade
Sieve/colander

The Bosch, designed for perfection, speed, efficiency, and ease of use, seems to be the most satisfactory of all household food processors. With the addition of the extra but essential meat grinder, it qualifies as a complete food processor. Double rotating whisks beat great quantities of air into eggs and cream and blend fine pastry doughs with a skill unexcelled by any other kitchen machine.

When operated manually, the three-pronged combination dough hook/folding attachment folds egg whites gently; when set on high speed, it kneads up to eight pounds of bread or yeast dough thoroughly.

The vegetable shredder/slicer attachment is exemplary. The round feed tube is easy to fill yet large enough to hold a whole onion for full slices; the blades are strong and sharp and produce professional results—the juliennes are splendid.

The wide, sturdy meat grinder is the best of all tested: it has four blades, including a very fine one for mousses and a coarse, sharp blade that chops carrots and onions; a large tray holds several pounds of cubed meat. The meat grinder requires no extra gear units: to operate, one simply turns the Bosch's U-shaped motor base on its side. Many of the accessories, including the pasta maker and fruit press, fit directly into the meat grinder, which keeps their cost, weight, and maintenance down.

The blender is one of the better ones tested. It chops well and is powerful; a funnel in the lid, for dripping liquids through, makes it ideal for sauce making. But, whereas the rest of the machine is made of the highest quality materials and looks as though it will last a lifetime, the blender is of a less than pleasing plastic and appears mismatched and temporary.

Otherwise, the individuals who designed the Bosch seem to have thought of almost everything: splash guards protect without obscuring one's view; a smooth, white cap, a safety feature, covers attachment units not in use and helps support the machine when it is turned on its side; when the base is upright, both attachment units can be used at once.

The Bosch is a handsome machine, built to last, and it performs all food processor functions without compromise. It is also extremely expensive, in a league with a well-equipped Kitchen Aid K5-A. The real drawback of the Bosch is not its price but its size. It is enormous and demands, in addition to an active household and a lively entertaining schedule, a truly spacious kitchen: it dwarfs ours, which is by no means small. Not only do the bowls and attachments require abundant storage space, but the base is so wide it cannot fit on standard width counters: size, not material, dictates that most parts be washed by hand. If cost and size are not deterrents, the Bosch seems to be the best all-around food processor available, ideal for anyone who really loves to cook and whose standards are high.

Braun® Kitchen Machine

L-shaped motor base with one gear attachment unit, spindle for holding mixing bowls
Glass blender, lid with feed tube, ¼-cup measure
4½-quart and 1½-quart plastic mixing bowls

- single whisk
- dough hook

Vegetable shredding/slicing attachment with large feed tube, one pusher, plus string bean cutter
5 shredding/slicing blades

(3 speeds plus manual)

Accessories:
  Meat grinder
  Juicer
  Coffee grinder

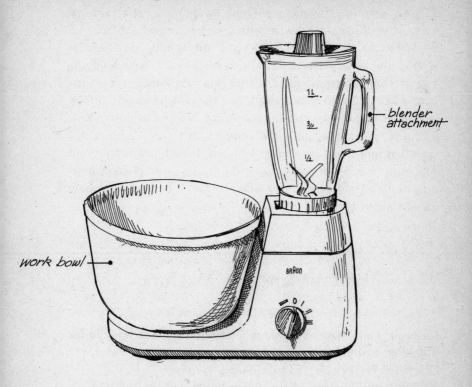

blender
attachment

work bowl

The Braun Kitchen Machine is sleek, beautiful, and spotlessly white. With the addition of the meat grinder attachment, an essential extra, the Braun performs all food processor functions completely and without compromise: grated carrots are long and firm; cucumber slices, regular and round; ground beef for hamburgers, just the right consistency. The L-shaped motor base, a good size to fit in all but the smallest kitchen, holds a mixing bowl and one attachment. Each Braun attachment is a precision instrument that one might consider purchasing separately. Combined, here is a complete food processor that is built to last: all is solid, orderly, precise.

The Braun is not a versatile and accessible machine, but an exacting one that requires care and some getting used to. Each attachment—the blender, the meat grinder, the vegetable shredder/slicer, and the dough hook and whisk—is equipped with its own gleaming stainless-steel gear unit that locks into place.

One must weigh the elegance of the Braun's clean lines, the importance of the fine work that it does, against the problems inherent in its maintenance and storage. Nothing is dishwasher safe; most attachments have several parts; cleaning, drying, and assembling can be burdensome.

The blender, while powerful and made of heavy glass, is too narrow: it holds only three cups of liquid without splattering; when chopping, ingredients must be turned over frequently with a rubber spatula. Though there are two mixing bowls, including one small enough for beating only two eggs, they are made of plastic, not stainless steel or glass.

The meat grinder is sturdy, serviceable, and powerful, though narrow and difficult to clean. Its single blade is perfect for pâtés; one grinds twice for steak tartare.

All in all, the Braun is a comprehensive household food processor that handles small quantities or large with finesse. The vegetable slicer/shredder produces fine results: the feed tube, though not ideal, can hold a single carrot or a small onion for whole round slices; the blades, which are easy to store, are of good quality, strong and sharp enough to grate pork fat for terrines.

Of all the attachments, the dough hook and whisk are probably the easiest to use: both fit into the same attachment arm and, though single and stationary, produce excellent results: egg whites are fluffy; pastry doughs, light. Since all attachments, save for the blender, feed into the mixing bowls, a large work surface is not required.

The Braun is quite reasonably priced and, though its performance is not in a league with the most expensive machines, it compares nicely with the Starmix and Oster Kitchen Center, the others of its type in the moderate price range. When one considers all the fine equipment the Braun Kitchen Machine offers, the quality of workmanship, and its superior design, the price tag seems modest.

Cuisinart™ Food Processor

Motor base with single drive shaft
Clear plastic work bowl with handle, lid with feed tube, pusher

- steel blade
- medium slicing blade; medium grating blade
- plastic blade for mixing

(One speed)

Accessories:
    Fine slicing blade
    Fine serrated slicing blade
    Fine grating blade
    French fry cutting blade

The Cuisinart, the food processor that almost single-handedly brought about the kitchen machine revolution, has broadened the realm of possibility for experienced cooks and fledglings alike. Dishes that were formerly fearsome—a homemade sausage en croûte, straw potatoes, a cold sole mousse—can now be made with ease in ordinary kitchens on a frequent, even last-minute, basis. Mayonnaises and Hollandaises, once the bane of longtime *sauciers*, have been transformed into lovely, light sauces that nearly anyone can master almost immediately.

The secret of the Cuisinart's success is not that it is the best food processor available, but that it is the most accessible, most versatile, and the easiest to use—in short, the most practical for day-to-day cooking.

Simplicity is the key to the Cuisinart. The same equipment is used whether chopping a single sprig of parsley, a duck for pâté, or fish for quenelles. All work is done in the wide, clear plastic work bowl, and almost all of it—be it blending sauces, kneading doughs, pureeing soups, grinding meats, grating cheeses or bread crumbs,

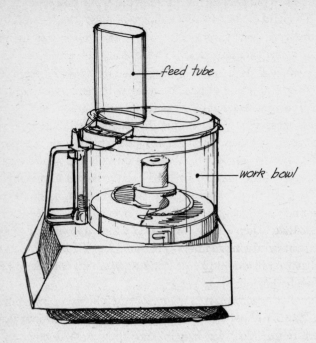

feed tube

work bowl

chopping onions, or mincing herbs—by the incredibly sharp double-edged steel blade. The steel blade chops with a precision unrivaled by any blender, save perhaps the Starmix; here, however, the sides rarely need to be scraped, and both bowl and blade can go right in the dishwasher. One never hesitates to use this food processor, even for a single onion.

Once the Cuisinart, small and powerful, is in place on the counter, it is set to go: the vegetable slicing and shredding blades fit right on the single drive shaft; there is only one feed tube for all processes; and there is nothing, save for blades,* to store, though a second work bowl—a highly worthwhile investment—will take up a bit of space.

The Cuisinart, like its archetype, the Robot Coupe, has only one

---

* We keep the plastic blade on the shelf except when mixing up a batch of chocolate chip cookies; for sauces and such, we prefer the familiarity of the steel blade.

speed which is operated by turning the work bowl on its motor base. To guard against overblending, one must watch carefully and turn the work bowl from side to side often, stopping from time to time to check on consistency. Though meat chopped by the steel blade will not have quite the same consistency as that pushed through a grinder, it is fine for most pâtés and mousses; texture can be regulated by chopping small quantities at a time.

The Cuisinart is not without its drawbacks. Though it shreds and slices vegetables with great speed, it does an uneven and less than perfect job. The feed tube is difficult and time-consuming to load, not wide enough to hold even a medium cucumber for whole round slices. Moreover, small vegetables, such as mushrooms and young carrots, tend to fall over midway down the feed tube so that, when slicing, one often winds up with a variegated assortment of shapes and sizes. The shredding blade is not as strong and sharp as we would like: it cannot grate hard cheeses; juliennes are flimsy.

Though the Cuisinart is marvelous at chopping and pureeing solids, it cannot hold more than two cups of liquid without leaking, making it less ideal for soup-making than a good blender. One final flaw: though the Cuisinart can mix eggs for the start of a sauce, it cannot beat air into eggs or cream, and it cannot fold. Fortunately, a reasonably priced electric beater can be acquired with ease from another source.

Despite a few compromises, the Cuisinart is the helping hand we would not want to be without. In all honesty, it *has* altered the way we cook: our gratinées are richer; our vegetables and salads more varied; our sauces, more elaborate. It is grand not to have to stop and think about setting up or cleaning whether slicing an onion or pulverizing shellfish for a Sauce Coulis.

The Cuisinart, a French import, belongs in the moderate price range, but until recently it had no true-to-form competition. The original, by the way, is a better, more solid, and more powerful machine than the newer arrivals.

Farberware® Food Processor

Motor base with single drive shaft
Clear plastic work bowl, lid with feed tube, pusher

- steel blade
- slicing blade; medium grating blade
- plastic blade for mixing

(One speed)

Accessories:
  None available as yet

At long last, the Cuisinart has real competition in the form of this Japanese-built kitchen machine that the American-based Farberware company launched in the late fall of 1976. Like its predecessor, the Farberware has a single clear plastic work bowl where all processing is done, four easy-to-fit blades, and a small

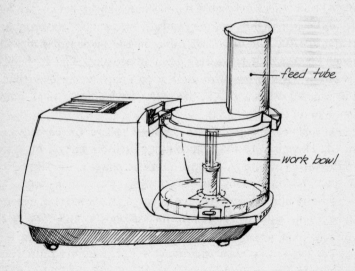

motor base. The Farberware requires no setting up and little storage space. It can do everything the Cuisinart can do, from grinding meat to blending sauces to kneading dough, and in the same manner. Like the original, the Farberware cannot beat air into eggs and creams and it cannot fold. An electric beater is an essential accessory to be purchased, at a reasonable price, from another source.

Since the Farberware is a rather faithful rendition of the Cuisinart, a comparison of the two seems warranted. In the Cuisinart, the motor is located directly under the drive shaft. In the Farberware, it is in the back and, thus, is not quite as efficient. The Farberware work bowl does not have a handle as does that of the luxury model Cuisinart, and it is a bit smaller; on the plus side, it does not leak as readily.

The blades are of comparable quality, though their diameters are slightly smaller. The flat, double-edged steel blade is strong and sharp and chops with great precision. The design of the grating blade is better than that of the Cuisinart; juliennes are long and firm. The slicing blade, as of now, produces slices that are a bit too thick, but we suspect that the engineers, who have already designed rubber feet to combat the machine's slight tremor, are hard at work on a slightly narrower blade. We should mention here that when the Cuisinart first came on the market, it had a few rough spots which have since been ironed out. The Farberware feed tube, though less than ideal, is an improvement over that of the original; it has a well in the center for holding a small potato or onion for full slices.

The main advantage that the Cuisinart has over the Farberware is speed. Though both food processors switch on and off by a turn of the work bowl, the Cuisinart has more power and a larger work surface and thus chops faster. The discrepancy increases as the work bowl fills up and the ingredients get harder: for instance, though four stalks of celery take four seconds to chop fine in the Cuisinart and five in the Farberware, it may take thirty to forty seconds longer to grate a work bowl full of stale bread into bread crumbs. In the grand scheme of things, we doubt these seconds are important, though they are an indication that the Cuisinart is the superior machine.

The Farberware offers convenience, simplicity, accessibility, and speed. It is a fine food processor for day-to-day cooking and entertaining and, were there not the original to compare it to, it would seem wondrous indeed. If you are conscious of your purse, the Farberware, which costs far less, seems the better buy. We think that anyone who wants a versatile, easy-to-clean kitchen machine without spending a fortune should think seriously about the Farberware.

Kitchen Aid® Model K5-A

Motor head with stand and base, basic attachment unit and accessory attachment unit, clamp for raising and lowering mixing bowl

5-quart stainless-steel mixing bowl

- rotary/revolving single balloon whisk
- rotary/revolving dough hook/folding attachment
- rotary/revolving flat pastry attachment/folding attachment

(10 speeds)

Accessories:
Rotary vegetable slicer/shredder with four blades
Vertical vegetable slicer/shredder with slicing blade; three grating blades and ice chipping blade
Meat grinder
Colander and sieve
Grain mill
Ice cream freezer

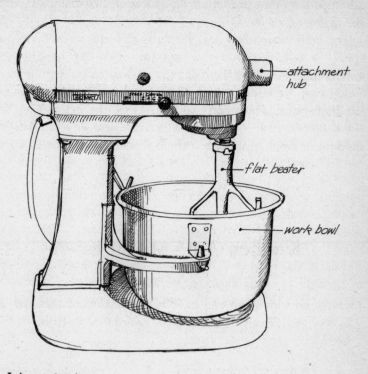

attachment hub

flat beater

work bowl

Juicer extractor
Sausage stuffer
Pour chute
Splash guard
Ice or hot water jacket
Can opener
Silver polisher

High on the list of exemplary kitchen machines is the Kitchen Aid, a sturdy, dependable, and expensive workhorse that gracefully executes feats so delicate serious bakers and sauce makers sing its praises. The Kitchen Aid is a heavy-duty, yet nimble, machine that is built to last a lifetime. It is easy to clean and maintain: the mixing bowl, the beaters, and the slicing/cutting blades can go right in the dishwasher. When two accessories—the meat grinder attachment and the vegetable cutter/slicer—are added, the Kitchen Aid performs *nearly* all food processor functions, and all of them with great skill. Though the range of accessories is vast, oddly enough a blender is not among them. Fortunately, one can be acquired from other sources with ease.

The basic K5-A, the quintessential mixing machine, consists of a baked enamel motor head and stand, a stainless-steel mixing bowl, and three easy-to-attach beaters. The K5-A takes up little counter space, is simple to operate and thoroughly accessible. The balloon whisk beats great quantities of air into eggs and cream, and, when in place, blends sauces smooth as silk. The flat pastry attachment mixes light doughs, mashes potatoes, folds egg whites, and is the recommended sauce maker. The dough hook kneads bread and yeast doughs, mixes heavy ingredients, and folds egg whites gently. Since the balloon whisk, with its revolving/rotating action, is wide and the mixing bowl deep and narrow, one rarely has to scrape the sides whether beating three eggs or twenty.

Though the K5-A's speeds correspond to the usual low, medium, and high—and thus are not difficult to get used to—with ten settings one can be sure of beating a chantilly slowly and gently and a meringue so briskly it stands up. The only bothersome feature of the K5-A is that, when in motion, there is too little space between the motor head and the mixing bowl so that pouring, even with the pour chute—an essential accessory—is precarious.

There is a separate accessory attachment unit at the front of the motor head, a design that enables one to use two attachments at once. The meat grinder, though old-fashioned looking, produces nicely textured ground meats and fish. The blades of both the vertical and the rotary vegetable slicer/cutter are sharp, strong, and precise; the feed tube is large enough to hold a whole onion for nice, round slices. Of the two types of vegetable attachments, we recommend the vertical model: the rotary cutter/slicer is a bit sluggish. Though the attachments are of good quality, they are quite costly. Moreover, some accessories are a bit difficult to attach and detach. Extra bowls for catching ground meat or sliced vegetables must be lined up in front of the machine's base, which requires a good deal of counter space. Since the attachments sit high, splattering can be a problem. When space and ease-of-use are issues, some cooks have chosen to complement their Kitchen Aid K5-A with a work bowl-type food processor, rather than with accessories since the costs are comparable. Other devotees of this stalwart machine prefer the far more professional results the Kitchen Aid accessories offer.

The K5-A is a marvelous machine for anyone who loves to bake or for anyone who enjoys cooking and entertaining and only wants to make so substantial a purchase once. Though far from pretty, the Kitchen Aid is a joy to use, and the results—from brioche doughs to humble slaws—are superb. The accessories, which range from a fine sieve/colander to a silver polisher, are among the best available and can be purchased over the years.

Oster® Kitchen Center™

Motor base with one gear attachment unit, 2 spindles and turn-table for holding mixing bowls

5-cup glass blender, lid with feed tube, ½-cup measure
4-quart and 1½-quart glass mixing bowls, mixer arm with handle

- 2 revolving beaters
- plastic meat grinder attachment with two blades

Accessories:
Vegetable shredding/slicing attachment with large feed tube plus feed guide for single carrot; chute·for continuous feed, 3 shredding/slicing blades
Dough maker arm with two dough hooks
Can opener
Citrus juicer

feed tube

work bowl

Cutting board
Ice crusher
Sausage maker

Among the most reasonably priced food processors is the Oster Kitchen Center, a thoroughly competent kitchen machine that calls for many separate attachments, all of them quite good. It has two sturdy glass bowls that rotate. The whisk attachment, an actual ten-speed mixer, mashes poatoes beautifully and whips eggs to a froth in no time. The mixer arm, which has a handle, lifts when work is done and ejects its two wide mixing blades. The large, powerful blender, though it does not chop with the speed and skill of the Starmix or Bosch, is splendid for making sauces and processing liquids; when filled to the top, it purees five cups of soup without spilling a drop.

We have had difficulty getting used to pushing buttons for various blender processes, such as "blend" or "liquefy," but if you have previously owned a pushbutton blender, perhaps this will not deter you. The "pulse" switch is helpful for redistributing bread crumbs and other light substances, though a rubber spatula is still requisite for carrots.

The meat grinder, though made of plastic and not metal, is powerful, short, wide, and easy to clean. Its two blades produce nicely textured meat and fish; the coarse blade grinds grain and nuts as well.

The Oster vegetable slicer/shredder or FoodCrafter, an extra but essential accessory, is outstanding—one of the best of all tested. Modeled after that of the Robot Coupe, the FoodCrafter has a compact base, three sharp disk blades, and a continuous feed chute for slicing and shredding in bulk. The feed tube is wide enough for slicing whole onions and deep enough so that even mushrooms and carrots can be sliced without falling over. A special slot allows carrots and celery to be sliced the long way. The julienne blade produces long, firm shreds and is strong enough to grate nuts and hard cheeses. In short, for processing vegetables for soups and such, the Oster vegetable slicer/shredder offers the accessibility and speed of a work bowl-type food processor.

The two rotating dough hooks do excellent work and knead bread and yeast doughs thoroughly, but they must be purchased, along with the dough maker arm, at extra cost. We wish it were not necessary to acquire the dough arm; it looks to be all but identical to the mixer arm, takes up extra space, and brings up the cost.

Much as we admire the performance of the Oster Kitchen Center, its cluttered appearance, mostly plastic with simulated wood trim, is not to our liking. Neither is the control panel base, which seems to defy common sense. Whereas all the other food processors operate quite simply by dialing a switch or turning a work bowl, with the Oster Kitchen Center, one must press an "on" button, adjust a power switch, and then—when using the ten-speed mixer, dough arm, or blender—start pressing buttons.

Otherwise we find the Oster Kitchen Center to be a fine all-purpose household food processor that can handle small quantities or large with equal ease. The base, which holds one attachment and a mixing bowl, will fit on any standard kitchen counter, though storage space is required. Best of all, even when fully equipped with the additional vegetable slicer/shredder attachment and the dough maker arm, the Oster Kitchen Center costs appreciably less than a comparably equipped Braun or Starmix, its closest competitors.

Robot Coupe Model R-2

Motor base with a single drive shaft for all parts and accessories
2½-quart plastic work bowl with splash guard

- double-edged steel blade
- medium slicing blade; grating blade

Vegetable shredder/slicer attachment with two feed tubes, pushers, and chute for continuous action

(One speed)

Accessories:
    Fine grating blade
    Coarse grating blade
    Fine slicing blade
    Waved potato slicing blade
    Julienne blade
    French fry cutting blade
    Juicer attachment

The Robot Coupe, one of the finest kitchen machines available, a favorite of restaurant owners, and the prototype for the Cuisinart, is built to process large quantities of food with speed and professional expertise. The Robot Coupe has a powerful motor that shuts off when overloaded, only one easy-to-operate speed, and only two basic attachments that sit on a single drive shaft.

The wide plastic work bowl, when fitted with the flat, double-edged steel blade, chops, grates, and purees vegetables; grinds

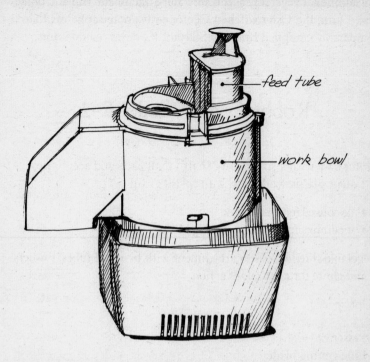

feed tube

work bowl

meats; and makes fine doughs and sauces. Though protected by a splash guard, the work bowl is open in the center, which makes pouring, filling, emptying, and cleaning easy. We find the opening a bit unnerving; supervision, especially if there are children around, is imperative.

The vertical vegetable shredder/slicer is excellent. It has two feed tubes, the smaller of which can hold a whole onion for perfect round slices; the larger, a half a head of cabbage for the world's fastest coleslaw. At the far end, there is a chute for the continuous flow of food. The blades are among the best available, and certainly the most precise—eight in all, each is labeled for a specific function; the waved potatoes are pure poetry.

Alas, the Robot Coupe is primarily for restaurants, catering establishments, and the rare private home where an elaborate dinner for ten or more is a weekly occurrence. Even Model R-2, the smallest—others process as much as forty quarts at a time—is better suited to chopping three onions than one, to making a Hollandaise for twelve than for two. The Robot Coupe, like its offshoot, cannot beat eggs and cream, and does not fold. The steel blade grinds meat, even veal, with incredible speed, but the texture is not quite that of meat pushed through a grinder.

This is an expensive machine, a commercial food processor that is designed to please the palate, not the eye—and on a large scale. The Robot Coupe is built for dependability, durability, easy access, and versatility. If yours is an extremely active, well-supervised kitchen in which speed and professional results are of great importance, the easy-to-use, easy-to-maintain Robot Coupe may well be worth its price tag.

Starmix MX 4

Motor base with one attachment unit for all basic parts and accessories
Glass blender, lid with feed tube, ¼-cup measure
5-quart stainless-steel mixing bowl, plastic splash guard

- double rotary whisk
- dough hook

Vegetable shredder/slicer attachment with two feed tubes, two pushers, plus string bean cutter
5 shredding/slicing blades

(2 speeds plus manual)

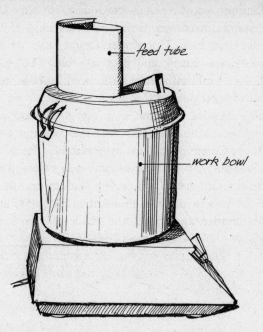

feed tube

work bowl

Accessories:
    Meat grinder attachment
    French fry cutter
    Ice cream freezer
    Juicer
    Juice extractor

The Starmix is a very compact, versatile kitchen machine. A single motor unit runs all the basic parts and takes up little counter space. The blender is powerful, the best of all tested. It makes perfect chopped ice in seconds and, when operated manually, chops onions quickly and evenly. The Starmix is an especially good choice for anyone interested in baking from scratch. The blender grinds rice or whole wheat kernels into flour; the dough hook kneads yeast doughs thoroughly; and the whisk makes lovely, light pastry doughs. The double rotary whisk is extraordinary: it swings around the sides of the deep stainless-steel mixing bowl so that one need rarely scrape the sides; as few as two egg whites can be beaten to a froth in no time.

The Starmix vegetable shredder/slicer attachment is not a success. Vegetables have to be forcibly pushed through the feed tube, a process far slower and more tedious than with other food processors; the blades do not seem to be as sharp or of as high quality as those of other machines; and the appearance of some vegetables, especially juliennes, suffers somewhat.

The Starmix is replete with good intentions gone awry. For instance, the splash guard is transparent but not open; though it provides protection against splattering, it also obscures one's view of sauces and such in preparation. Similarly, though the vegetable shredder/slicer has two feed tubes, the smaller is a fine size for a single carrot, but the larger is too narrow to hold even a whole small onion for round slices. Moreover, though the Starmix is mostly dishwasher safe, easy to maintain, and made of high-quality materials, it is not attractive.

The Starmix is a good food processor for a small kitchen, and fine for anyone who likes to blend, chop, grind, bake, and whip eggs and cream—and only occasionally slice and shred. It is competitively priced, though the meat grinder, an essential part, is extra.

Instructions for Using This Cookbook

Here, we offer recipes and instructions for using the food processor. At the start of each recipe, we list the food processor blades and accessories required to complete a dish, in their order of use. Equipment needed will vary according to the type of food processor owned. Usually, those with separate attachments will require a blender and either a meat grinder or a whisk attachment. Those with work bowls will nearly always call for the steel blade. If there are eggs or cream to be beaten, we list "hand beater" at the top, since these machines have no whisk attachments. Since both types of food processors have vegetable slicing and shredding blades, though not all have special vegetable slicer/shredder attachments, we call only for the blades.

In general, the attachments and blades listed are those that are common to most food processors. Should you have a wider range of slicing and shredding blades, specialized attachments, or extra bowls, please feel free to use the equipment and methods you like best. Here, as with any other cookbook, it is wise to read a recipe all the way through before attempting it. We have tried to write the recipes in an informative step-by-step manner so that, even if you are new to your food processor, the directions will be easy to follow. Whenever you have questions, please refer to the list of SPECIAL INSTRUCTIONS for your food processor at the front of this book. Mark it with a ribbon and turn to it often. Below, we list three frequently used terms that may be confusing:

[24]

Feed tube: Any opening through which one feeds food to be processed. Feed tubes include the opening in the cover of the work bowl; any opening in which vegetables to be sliced or shredded are placed; and the opening in the blender lid through which liquid can be poured.

Work bowl: The wide, all-purpose bowl of the Cuisinart, the Farberware, and the Robot Coupe, in which almost all processing is done.

Mixing bowl: That bowl—made of glass, stainless steel, or plastic —which fits on a blender-type food processor and is used in conjunction with the whisk or pastry attachment.

Frequently used ingredients, including *chopped parsley, bread crumbs,* and *grated cheese,* can be processed in quantity in the food processor and sealed and stored in the refrigerator. We do not give instructions for preparing these in the recipes, since we assume you will already have them on hand or can process them with ease. Please check your food processor manual and our list of SPECIAL INSTRUCTIONS for the best and easiest methods of chopping parsley, grating bread crumbs, and grating hard cheeses with your food processor.

Hors d'oeuvres

Hot Hors d'oeuvres

Sausage en Croûte

This spicy, dough-wrapped sausage, much like cotechino, a favorite Italian garlic sausage, is not at all difficult to make. Each part, as well as the entire dish, may be prepared in advance and frozen. We enter the recipe for mixed spices here. Once made up, the mixed spices will keep for a year, and can be used for seasoning all your pâtés and sausages.

Sausage en Croûte can be served hot or cold, with Dijon mustard or without. If you want to serve this winter dish as a main course, double the quantities for sausage and dough, and make the sausage twice as fat.

Note: If your food processor has a sausage-stuffing attachment, you may choose to grind the seasoned meat directly into natural casings. The sausage can then be boiled in red wine or broth for 45 minutes; be sure to prick the casing first.

HOMEMADE SAUSAGE EN CROÛTE

Mixed Spices
(BLENDER OR STEEL BLADE, OR, IF YOU PREFER, COFFEE MILL)

On the shelf of every serious sausage maker is a jar of mixed spices, a classic blend that enhances all forcemeats from the finest rillettes to the coarsest country pâtés. This mixture can be made up all at once, stored in a tightly sealed container, and used throughout the year. The character of your pâté or sausage will be determined, to a great extent, by the spices you select. If you are fond of garlic, add one or two cloves to your sausage meat (see recipe below).

Ingredients

1 tablespoon each:
Bay leaf
Clove
Mace
Nutmeg
Paprika
Thyme

1½ tablespoons each:
Basil
Cinnamon
Marjoram or Oregano
Sage
Savory

½ cup:
White peppercorns

Place all the spices in the blender, work bowl, or coffee mill. Grind the spices for 3 or 4 minutes, until they form a fine powder.
Strain the spices through a very fine sieve. Seal and store.

The Sausage
(MEAT GRINDER OR STEEL BLADE)

Ingredients

2 garlic cloves (optional)
1 pound lean fresh pork, cut
　　into 1½-inch pieces
1 pound fresh pork fat (see
　　Note on page 31), cut
　　into 1½-inch pieces

1 tablespoon mixed spices
　　(see page 29)
Salt and pepper to taste

Mince the garlic and set aside.
Push the pork and pork fat through the meat grinder, or, if using

the steel blade, place the pork in the work bowl and run the food processor for 2½ minutes; remove the pork to a bowl. Add the pork fat to the work bowl and run for 1 minute, or until it forms a paste. Add the fat to the ground pork.

To the ground meat, add the mixed spices and the minced garlic cloves. Add salt and pepper to taste. Mix well with your hands, or, if you prefer, a wooden spoon.

To test for seasonings before you form your sausage, make a tiny meat ball and poach it in boiling water for 1 minute. Taste and correct the seasonings.

Note: Ask the butcher for pure pork fat. Fresh fatback or salted fatback may be substituted, but neither dissolves quite as well as fresh pork fat. If using salted fatback (available at most supermarkets), blanch it first in boiling water to remove the salt. Drain, pat dry, and remove the rind.

The Dough
(WHISK ATTACHMENT OR STEEL OR PLASTIC BLADE)

This multipurpose never-fail dough is at its best wrapped around sausages, pâtés, a whole striped bass, or a fillet of beef. It can be used to make the shells for hors d'oeuvres tarts and tartlets, or, by replacing the salt with 1 tablespoon of sugar, for sweet pie-crusts. We have tested making this dough many different ways and find that if we simply put all the ingredients in the food processor, taking care not to run the machine too long, the results are excellent. Note that the proportions of butter, oil, and water are equal. The dough may be stored overnight in the refrigerator or frozen.

Ingredients

½ cup melted butter
½ cup hot water
½ cup vegetable oil

4 cups flour
Pinch of salt

Place all the ingredients in the work bowl or mixing bowl and run the food processor for 2½ minutes or until the dough is a coarse meal; pat together to form a ball.

Dust the dough with flour and let it stand in a cool place while you prepare the sausage meat.

Assembling the sausage en croûte:

Ingredients

Dough	1 egg and 1 tablespoon water,
Sausage meat	mixed

Preheat the oven to 375°.

Flour a board and roll the dough into an ⅛-inch-thick rectangle, approximately 8 x 11 inches.

Wet your hands and shape the meat into a fairly narrow sausage shape.

Place the meat in the center of the dough and wrap the dough around the sausage. Seal the edges with water as you would seal an envelope.

Place the wrapped sausage, seam side down, on a buttered baking sheet.

With the excess dough, make a design and decorate the crust; moisten the decorations with water so that they stick to the dough.

Brush the dough with the egg-and-water mixture.

Cook the sausage for 35 minutes, or until the pastry is shiny and golden brown.

Serve whole on a platter decorated with watercress, or slice and serve on individual plates.

Yield: 8 to 10 servings

Two Stuffed Mushroom Caps

Mushrooms worthy of stuffing are large, white, and firm. They should look as beautiful as they taste. To keep them full and white, set the caps in a bowl of water with 1 tablespoon of lemon juice or vinegar. When a mushroom is very fresh, it is easy to tear the cap while removing the stem. To avoid this, we suggest using the tip of a dessert spoon to dig around the stem; then break off the stem.

MUSHROOMS STUFFED WITH CLAMS
(BLENDER OR STEEL BLADE)

Ingredients

8–10 large, fresh mushrooms
1 tablespoon lemon juice or
    vinegar
1 dozen cherrystone clams or
    one 10-ounce can of clams,
    drained
2 scallions, trimmed
1 garlic clove

2 sprigs fresh dill, or ¼
    teaspoon dried dill
6 tablespoons butter
2 tablespoons bread crumbs
Salt and pepper to taste
1 tablespoon chopped parsley
3 large tomatoes (optional)

Preheat the oven to 275°.

Wash the mushroom caps and place in a bowl of water with lemon juice or vinegar.

Remove the stems carefully, pat them dry, and reserve for chopping.

Place the cherrystone clams in a 275° oven for 5 minutes or until the shells open. Remove the clams from the shells. (If using canned clams, drain well.)

Raise the oven heat to 350°.

Place the clams in the blender or work bowl. Add the scallions, garlic, and dill, and run the food processor for 3 seconds. Remove the mixture to a bowl.

Add the mushroom stems to the blender or work bowl and run the food processor for 2 seconds. Set aside.

In a heavy skillet, heat 4 tablespoons of butter. When the butter is bubbling, add the clam mixture and sauté for 2 minutes, stirring frequently with a wooden spoon.

Add the mushroom stems to the skillet and continue stirring for 3 more minutes.

Off the heat, add the bread crumbs. Add salt and pepper to taste.

Drain the mushroom caps and pat dry. Set the remaining butter on the stove to melt.

Fill the mushroom caps with the clam mixture.

Place the mushroom caps on a buttered baking dish and brush melted butter over the filling.

Bake in a preheated 350° oven for 10 minutes until the butter is bubbling.

Sprinkle with chopped parsley. If serving as a first course, place each mushroom cap on a slice of ripe tomato.

Yield: 4 servings

ESCARGOTS IN MUSHROOM CAPS
(BLENDER OR STEEL BLADE)

Ingredients

24 snails, canned, drained, and patted dry
24 large, white, firm mushroom caps
1 cup parsley, tightly packed

5 garlic cloves
1 stick butter, cut in small pieces
Salt and pepper to taste

Preheat the broiler.

Prepare mushroom caps for stuffing (see page 33).

Add the parsley, garlic, and butter to the blender or work bowl. Run the food processor for 5 seconds. Season with salt and pepper to taste.

Place one escargot or snail in each mushroom cap. Cover the escargot with the garlic-and-parsley butter. Do not butter the base of the mushroom cap; it should remain hard.

Place the mushroom caps on a baking sheet and broil for 10 minutes until the butter is bubbling.

Serve immediately.

Yield: 4 to 6 servings

Two Crepes

Hors d'oeuvres crepes, thin slips of pancake especially for filling, are soft and light. These are delightful wrapped around the elegant and piquant stuffings listed below, or filled with leftover meat and covered with a cream sauce.

THE CREPE
(BLENDER OR STEEL OR PLASTIC BLADE)

Ingredients

3 eggs
½ cup heavy cream
½ cup milk
6 tablespoons flour

⅛ teaspoon salt
4 tablespoons melted butter
    plus 1 pat butter for pan

In the blender or work bowl, place the eggs, cream, milk, flour, salt, and butter. Run the food processor for 8 seconds. Pour the batter into a bowl and let it stand, covered, for 1 hour.

Melt the pat of butter in a crepe pan. When the butter bubbles, pour in 3 tablespoons of batter and quickly tilt and rotate the pan until the batter covers the entire surface.

When the edges are lightly browned, turn the crepe with a spatula and heat the other side for only a few seconds. Slide the crepe onto a dish.

Without rebuttering the pan, pour 3 more tablespoons of batter into the crepe pan and continue making crepes until you have used up all the batter.

Yield: 12 to 16 crepes

Note: Crepes can be made up to a day in advance. To keep, slide the crepes onto a large sheet of waxed paper, cut the paper into squares, stack, cover, and refrigerate.

CREPES WITH SMOKED SALMON
(SHREDDING BLADE; BLENDER OR STEEL BLADE)

This lively summer dish makes a wonderful prelude to an otherwise simple dinner. It is especially good at noon with an arugula or tomato salad.

Ingredients

12–16 crepes (see page 35)
2 cups Hollandaise Sauce (see page 173)*
4 hard-boiled eggs
6 ounces smoked salmon

2 tablespoons fresh dill sprigs or 1 tablespoon dried dill
Salt and pepper to taste
4 tablespoons grated Parmesan cheese
2 tablespoons butter

Preheat the oven to 375°.

In the blender or work bowl, place the eggs, the salmon, and the dill. Run the food processor for 6 seconds. Add salt and pepper, robustly, to taste and mix well with a wooden spoon.

Spread the filling down the center of each crepe. Roll the crepes and place them, seam side down, on a buttered baking dish.†

Bake the crepes in a preheated 375° oven for 10 minutes.†

Remove the dish from the oven. Pour the Hollandaise Sauce over the crepes and sprinkle with the grated Parmesan.

Dot the crepes with butter and broil for a few minutes until golden brown.

Yield: 4 to 6 servings

* You can make Hollandaise Sauce at any point in the recipe. If you prepare the sauce ahead, place it in a dish of tepid water to keep it from separating.
† It is quite simple, once you have prepared the crepes and filling, to stuff and roll the crepes at the last minute. However, if you prefer, the crepes can be prepared to either of these points a day in advance and kept, well sealed, in the refrigerator. Do not freeze the crepes or they will become soggy.

CREPES STUFFED WITH MUSHROOMS
(BLENDER OR STEEL BLADE)

This luxuriant mushroom filling, often called *duxelles*, is a lovely concoction to have on hand to add to a gravy or sauce or to slide under the skin of a roasting chicken. Since it is called for in many recipes, you may prefer to prepare duxelles in large quantities to store in your refrigerator for future use; it will keep for three weeks. If so, *before* you cook the mushrooms, be sure to squeeze all the liquid out. To do this, after you wash and dry the mushrooms, place them, a small handful at a time, in a dish towel and wring until every drop of water is out. The recipe below is very quick, and the results, though fleeting, are wonderful.

Ingredients

12–16 crepes (see page 35)   3 tablespoons chopped parsley
1 pound firm, white mushrooms   Salt and pepper to taste
4 small shallots   1½ cups Béchamel Sauce
1 medium onion, quartered   (see page 182)
4 tablespoons butter   3 tablespoons grated Parmesan
2 tablespoons oil   cheese

Clean the mushrooms carefully, drain, and pat dry.

Place the mushrooms, shallots, and onion in the blender or work bowl and run the food processor for 5 seconds. Remove to bowl.

Heat 2 tablespoons of butter and the oil in a heavy skillet. When it is very hot, add the mushroom-and-onion mixture. Continue cooking over a high flame, stirring continuously with a wooden spoon until all the water from the mushrooms has evaporated.

Add the chopped parsley. Season with salt and pepper to taste and stir. Set the skillet on the side of the stove to cool.*

When the mushrooms have cooled, spread the filling down the center of each crepe. Roll the crepes and place them, seam side down, on a buttered baking dish.*

If not already prepared, make the Béchamel Sauce.

Bake the crepes in a preheated 375° oven for 10 minutes.*

Remove dish from the oven. Pour the Béchamel Sauce over the crepes and sprinkle with grated Parmesan.

Dot with the remaining butter and place under the broiler until golden brown.

Serve crepes at once, decorated with parsley sprigs.

Yield: 6 to 8 first-course servings

---

* This dish may be prepared to any of these points several hours in advance. When reheating crepes, dot with butter.

WALNUT OMELET
(BLENDER OR STEEL BLADE)

This flavorful and unusual omelet, at its best in the fall when walnuts are fresh, is cooked without folding and is served, like a cake, cut in wedges. It is delicious at midday with an arugula salad. Since the nutmeat is quite sweet, season vigorously with salt and pepper.

Ingredients

20 whole walnuts, shelled
8 eggs
4 tablespoons butter

Salt and pepper, heavily, to taste
1 tablespoon chopped parsley

Blanch the walnuts for 5 minutes in boiling water to loosen the skin. Remove the skin.*

Place the walnuts in the blender or work bowl and run the food processor for 8 seconds, or until the nutmeat is the texture of granulated sugar. You may have to stop the food processor several times to scrape the nutmeat away from the blades with a rubber spatula.

With the food processor running, drop the eggs, one at a time, through the feed tube. Beat till the eggs are well mixed and frothy, 5 seconds more at most.†

Heat the butter in a heavy 8- or 9-inch skillet and, when it is bubbling, add the egg-and-walnut mixture.

Add salt and pepper to taste. Correct the seasonings.

To be sure that the omelet, which should be quite high and fluffy, cooks evenly, lift the edges from time to time and with a

---

* The walnuts can be shelled, blanched, and skinned in advance, even the night before. This step can easily take 25 minutes.

† Beware of blending this or any other egg mixture too long, or the results will be dense instead of light and fluffy. If the mixture separates, turn the food processor on for a fraction of a second.

spatula make a slit or two near the center so that any liquid egg can be evenly distributed in the skillet.

After 2 minutes, or when the bottom is well set, turn the omelet onto a plate. Slide the omelet back onto the skillet and cook for another few minutes to suit your taste.

Slide the omelet onto a platter and sprinkle with chopped parsley. Serve at once.

To turn the omelet: Place a large plate over the skillet so that it forms a lid, and, holding the plate, turn the skillet upside down. Right the skillet and place it back on the burner. Slide the omelet from the plate onto the skillet and continue cooking.

Yield: 4 servings

Two Quiches

Quiche is always filled with an egg-and-cream custard to which other ingredients—cheese, onions, spinach, lobster, tomatoes, or crabmeat—are added. The shell of pâte brisée, a rich butter dough, is especially well suited to salted pies and small tarts. It can be converted into a fine sweet piecrust by replacing the salt with 1 tablespoon of sugar.

When making pâte brisée, be careful not to mix the dough too long. When raw, the dough should be smooth and resilient; if you beat it too long in the food processor, the dough will break apart and become sticky. Should this happen, stop the food processor and add 2 tablespoons of flour. Then run the machine for 10 more seconds and stop; the pâte brisée should be just right.

PÂTE BRISÉE
(WHISK ATTACHMENT OR STEEL BLADE)

Ingredients

1¾ cups flour
1 stick butter, chilled and cut
  in pieces
¼ teaspoon salt

1 egg
1 tablespoon oil
¼ cup ice water

In the mixing bowl or work bowl, place the flour, butter, and salt. Run the food processor for 20 seconds, or until the mixture forms a coarse meal.

In a small pitcher or measuring cup, combine the egg, oil, and ice water. Start the food processor and pour the liquid through the feed tube in a steady stream. Continue running the food processor for 20 seconds and stop.

Make a ball of the dough. Wrap it in waxed paper and chill it in the refrigerator for 1 hour, or until it is firm and ready to be used. The dough will keep for several days in the refrigerator or it can be frozen.

To make the quiche shell:

Preheat the oven to 400°.

When the dough is chilled, roll it on a floured board and fit into a 9-inch tart pan, preferably with a removable bottom.*

Prick the dough with a fork and line with waxed paper. Cover the bottom with enough raw rice to keep the shell from rising.

Bake in a preheated 400° oven until the dough is cooked but not brown. Remove from the oven and reserve; the quiche shell is now ready to be filled.

---

* The shell may be made ahead to this point and will keep for a day in the refrigerator, or for several weeks if frozen.

QUICHE LORRAINE
WITH ONIONS AND BACON
(SHREDDING BLADE; BLENDER OR STEEL BLADE)

Ingredients

1 9-inch quiche shell (see page 41)

1 medium onion, quartered

6 slices of bacon, cut in several pieces

1 tablespoon butter

2 whole eggs plus 1 egg yolk

½ cup milk

¼ cup heavy cream

¼ teaspoon salt

2 tablespoons grated Gruyère cheese

Preheat the oven to 375°.

Place the onion and bacon in the blender or work bowl and run the food processor for 3 seconds.

Heat the butter in a heavy skillet. Add the chopped onion and bacon, and cook over a medium-high heat until the bacon is crisp. Drain on paper towels.

Without washing the blender or work bowl, add the eggs, milk, heavy cream, and salt. Run the food processor for 4 seconds, or until the custard is fluffy.

Spread the chopped bacon and onion on the bottom of the tart shell. Sprinkle grated Gruyère over the mixture.

Pour the custard layer on top.

Place the quiche on a baking sheet in a preheated 375° oven and bake for 30 minutes until the filling is set and the top is golden. To test if the custard is set, insert a needle into it. If the needle comes out clean, the quiche is just right; if not, bake for a few more minutes and test again.

Yield: 6 to 8 slices

QUICHE WITH TOMATOES, ANCHOVIES, AND HERBS
(SHREDDING BLADE; BLENDER OR STEEL BLADE)

This tart, with its Provençal origins, is surprisingly light and delicate. Most of its flavor comes from the herb-and-custard filling; the tomatoes, anchovies, and parsley lend coloring. Pitted Greek olives and capers may be substituted for anchovies.

Ingredients

1 9-inch quiche shell (see page 41)
¼ cup grated Swiss cheese
¼ cup grated Parmesan cheese
1 cup heavy cream
½ cup light cream
2 eggs plus 2 egg yolks
1½ cups tomato puree (see page 44)
½ teaspoon salt
¼ teaspoon freshly ground white pepper
4 ripe tomatoes
1 can anchovies, drained and cut in pieces
2 tablespoons chopped parsley

Preheat the oven to 375°.

Grate the cheeses. Remove to a bowl.

In the blender or work bowl, place all the cream, eggs, tomato puree, and salt and pepper. Run the machine for 4 seconds, or until the mixture is quite frothy.

Fill the tart shell with the mixture.

Slice the tomatoes into ½-inch slices and set in a circle slightly overlapping on top of the mixture. Place two or three pieces of anchovy on each tomato slice. Sprinkle the quiche with chopped parsley and the grated cheeses.

Bake on a baking sheet in a preheated 375° oven for 35 minutes, or until the filling is set and the tomatoes cooked but not wilted. Serve piping hot.

Yield: 6 first-course servings

Fresh Tomato Puree
(BLENDER OR STEEL BLADE)

Ingredients

4 or 5 large tomatoes
1 medium onion, quartered
Sprig of parsley
¼ teaspoon thyme
1 bay leaf

2 tablespoons butter
Pinch of sugar
½ teaspoon salt
¼ teaspoon pepper

Quarter the tomatoes and remove the seeds.

Place the tomatoes in the blender or work bowl and run the food processor for 10 seconds. Remove tomatoes to a bowl.

Place the quartered onion in the blender or work bowl and run the food processor for 10 seconds, or until the onion is minced. Add the parsley, thyme, and bay leaf, and run for 2 more seconds.

Heat the butter in a heavy skillet and, when it is hot, add the tomatoes and the onion-and-herb mixture. Stir briefly.

To the skillet, add the sugar, salt, and pepper. Cover and cook the mixture over a low heat for 10 minutes.

Remove the cover and, stirring with a wooden spoon, continue to cook the mixture over a high heat for 4 or 5 minutes until the tomato puree forms a thick paste.

Yield: 1½ to 2 cups

Note: This tomato puree, stuffed into hard-boiled egg whites or raw mushroom caps, can be used to decorate a platter of pork roast, pot roast, or cold meats.

Three Puff Shells,
Stuffed and Sauced
(WHISK ATTACHMENT OR STEEL OR PLASTIC BLADE)

When we speak of puff shells, we usually mean shiny golden puffs, 2 inches across, which, when elaborately stuffed and sauced, can only be eaten sitting down. But puff pastry, or pâte à choux, is wonderfully versatile. With two dessert spoons, we can shape it into tiny puffs, the size of walnuts, to be filled with duxelles or cold shrimp, and passed with drinks. Or, by rolling the dough flat, we can make lighter-than-air cheese sticks simply by sprinkling the pâte à choux with grated Parmesan, cutting it into thin sticks, and brushing the sticks with a mixture of egg and water. By adding 1 tablespoon of sugar instead of salt, pâte à choux can be transformed into shells for cream puffs, eclairs, and other sweet desserts.

PÂTE À CHOUX
OR PUFF PASTRY DOUGH
(WHISK ATTACHMENT OR STEEL OR PLASTIC BLADE)

Ingredients

4 tablespoons butter, cut in
  6 pieces
⅔ cup water

Pinch of salt
1 cup flour
5 large eggs

Preheat the oven to 425°.

In a saucepan, place the butter, water, and salt, and bring to a boil.

When the butter is melted, add the flour *all at once*. Stir quickly with a wooden spoon.

Continue to stir until the dough clings together in a mass, completely free from the sides of the pan.

When the dough clings together, place it in the mixing bowl or work bowl, and run the food processor for 15 seconds. Stop the machine.

Add 1 egg to the dough. Run the food processor for a few seconds until the egg is absorbed in the dough. Stop the machine, and repeat the process with 3 additional eggs. When the dough is thick and shiny, the pâte à choux is ready to use.*

To make puff shells:

Fill a pastry bag with pâte à choux, or use two soup spoons dipped in cold water to make dough balls an inch in diameter and a half inch high.

Drop the dough balls onto a buttered baking sheet, leaving 2 inches between each one; the puff shells will expand as they bake.

Beat 1 egg plus ½ teaspoon of water together. Brush each dough ball with this mixture.

Bake in a preheated 425° oven for 20 minutes.

When the puff shells are golden brown, remove the baking sheet from the oven. Slit the side of each puff shell with a sharp knife, so that it remains hinged on one side, like a clam shell.

Place the puff shells back in the oven and turn off the heat. Let the pastry shells sit for 10 minutes until the inside dough is dry.

Yield: 12 to 14 puff shells

---

* Puff shells can be made as far in advance as the night before. They can be refrigerated.

PUFF SHELLS WITH SWEETBREADS
AND SAUCE PIQUANTE

An unusual accompaniment to pastry shells, these tender sweetbreads in their lemony sauce make a superb first course or late-night supper. Both the puff shells and the Sauce Piquante call for the aid of the food processor, though the filling does not.

Ingredients

12–14 puff shells (see page 45)
4 pairs of sweetbreads
¼ cup lemon juice or
   1 tablespoon vinegar
6 tablespoons butter

Salt and pepper to taste
Sauce Piquante (see
   page 194)*
Parsley for decoration

Preheat the oven to 375°.

Clean the sweetbreads by soaking in a bowl of cold water for 2 hours, changing the water several times.

Drain the sweetbreads and place them in a saucepan with water to cover. Add lemon juice or vinegar and bring the liquid to a boil. Simmer for 20 minutes.

In a colander, rinse the sweetbreads under cold water and drain.

With a paring knife, cut away the connecting tissues and membranes, leaving only the soft meat.

Slice the sweetbreads into ⅓-inch slices.

In a skillet, heat the butter. When it is hot, add the sweetbreads and sauté them for 10 minutes. Add salt and pepper to taste.

At serving time, add the sweetbreads to the Sauce Piquante and heat. Spoon the filling into the slitted puff shells. Decorate with parsley and serve immediately.

Yield: 6 first-course servings

* Sauce Piquante may be prepared at any point and will keep for several hours in a bowl set in tepid water.

PUFF SHELLS WITH
BAY SCALLOPS AND MORELS
(BLENDER OR STEEL BLADE)

Morels, quite dear, are heavenly and worth searching for in your specialty food shops. It is rare to find fresh morels in this country but, if you do find some, treasure them *and* wash them carefully. If you cannot locate dried imported morels, you can substitute dried Chinese mushrooms.

Ingredients

12–14 puff shells (see page 45)
6 ounces morels, dried
4 tablespoons butter
1 pound bay scallops (or
   1 pound sea scallops,
   quartered), washed and
   patted dry (see Note on
   page 49)

1 tablespoon tarragon
Salt and pepper to taste
2 tablespoons cognac
1 cup Béarnaise Sauce (see
   page 174)*

Preheat the oven to 375°

Rinse the dried morels in cold water. Soak them for 30 minutes in hot water to which 1 tablespoon of salt has been added.

Drain the morels and dry carefully with paper towels. Place them in the blender or work bowl and chop for 3 seconds.

In a heavy skillet, heat the butter. When it is hot, add the morels and sauté for 3 minutes until they are light brown.

Add the scallops to the skillet. Add the tarragon, and salt and pepper to taste. Cook, over medium heat, for 8 to 10 minutes until the scallops are still firm but easily pierced with a fork.

Remove from heat, pour cognac over the scallops, and ignite.

Add the Béarnaise Sauce to the scallops and mix well. Taste and correct the seasonings.

* Béarnaise Sauce can be prepared at any point in the recipe. If you make it ahead, reserve it in a bowl set in tepid water.

At serving time, fill the slitted puff shells with the scallops in Béarnaise Sauce. Heat in a 375° oven for 5 minutes. Serve immediately.

Yield: 6 first-course servings

Note: To keep scallops fresh, wash them and set in a bowl of cold running water. When you are ready to use them, drain and dry well with paper towels.

PUFF SHELLS WITH CRABMEAT AND LEMON CAPER SAUCE
(BLENDER OR STEEL BLADE)

Ingredients

12–14 puff shells (see page 45)
½ pound ham
1 medium onion, quartered
½ large green pepper, seeded
1 large garlic clove
4 tablespoons butter
3 tablespoons oil

1½ pounds crabmeat, picked
    over to remove shells
⅓ cup cognac
2 cups Lemon Caper Sauce
    (see page 193)*
1 teaspoon salt
1 teaspoon pepper

Preheat the oven to 375°.

In the blender or work bowl, place the ham, onion, green pepper, and garlic. Run the food processor for 2 minutes.

In a heavy skillet, melt the butter and oil. When the butter is melted, add the ham-and-onion mixture and cook, over medium heat, for 5 minutes, or until the onions are soft.

Add the crabmeat to the skillet and stir, cooking only until the crabmeat is heated through. Add the cognac and flame.

---

* Lemon Caper Sauce may be prepared several hours in advance. Set in a bowl in tepid water to keep sauce from separating.

Pour the crab mixture into the Lemon Caper Sauce. Stir. Add salt and pepper to taste.

At serving time, fill the slitted puff shells with the crab in Lemon Caper Sauce and heat in a 375° oven for 5 minutes.

Yield: 6 first-course servings

SALMON SOUFFLÉ
(BLENDER OR STEEL BLADE; WHISK ATTACHMENT OR HAND BEATER; FOLDING ATTACHMENT, IF AVAILABLE)

This soufflé, fragrant with dill, can be made with striped bass or halibut instead of salmon. Use a 1-quart buttered soufflé dish, and decorate with slices of lemon and lime.

Court Bouillon

Ingredients

1 fish head	4 peppercorns
2½ cups water	1 bay leaf
1 medium onion, whole	1 pound salmon
1 tablespoon lemon juice	

In a large saucepan, add the fish head and all the other ingredients except for the salmon.

Bring to a boil. Reduce the heat and simmer, covered, for 10 minutes.

Add the salmon to the bouillon and poach, covered, in the simmering liquid for 8 minutes. The salmon is done when the flesh turns pink and flakes easily when tested with a fork.

Using two spatulas so the fish doesn't break, remove the salmon to a platter to cool.

When cool enough to handle, remove the skin from the salmon

and discard. Separate the flesh from the bone, and place the meat in a bowl. Look salmon over carefully to be sure that there are no bones left. Reserve.

Pour the bouillon through a strainer into a small saucepan. Over a high heat, reduce the bouillon to three quarters of a cup. Set aside.

Salmon Soufflé

Ingredients

¾ cup of Court Bouillon (see page 50)
1 pound cooked salmon (see page 50)
¼ cup fresh dill, tightly packed, or 2 tablespoons dried dill
3 tablespoons flour

5 tablespoons butter
½ teaspoon dry mustard
3 egg yolks
Salt and pepper to taste
4 egg whites
1 lemon and 1 lime, sliced thin, for garnish

Preheat the oven to 375°.

Place the dill in the blender or work bowl and run the food processor for 5 seconds or until it is chopped fine. Set aside.

Wipe out the blender or work bowl and add the flour and 3 tablespoons of butter, cut in small pieces. Run the food processor for 4 seconds. Stop the machine.

With the food processor running, pour the Court Bouillon through the feed tube; this will take approximately 3 seconds. Stop the machine.

Add the dry mustard to the Court Bouillon and run the food processor for 2 seconds. Remove the mixture to a saucepan.

Over a medium flame, bring the mixture to a boil, stirring constantly until you have a thick white sauce. The sauce is ready when it sticks to a wooden spoon. Add salt and pepper to taste. Reserve.

Place the 3 egg yolks in the blender or work bowl and run the food processor for 2 seconds. Add the chopped dill; run the food processor for 1 second.

Add the cooked salmon to the egg yolks and run the food processor for 2 seconds, or until you have a thick paste.

Now, pour the salmon mixture slowly into the reserved white sauce, stirring with a wooden spoon. Add more salt and pepper if necessary. Let the mixture cool.

With the remaining butter, grease a 1-quart soufflé dish. Pour the egg whites into the mixing bowl and beat with the whisk attachment or an electric beater until very stiff.

Using a wooden spoon, fold one quarter of the egg whites into the salmon mixture, folding carefully so as not to break the whites. Then, slowly pour the salmon mixture into the remaining egg whites, folding slowly and gently so that the soufflé, when cooked, will be streaked with white.*

Pour the soufflé mixture into the buttered soufflé dish. Bake, on a baking sheet, in a preheated 375° oven for 45 minutes.

When the soufflé is puffed high and golden brown, it is ready. Garnish with alternate slices of lemon and lime and serve immediately.

Yield: 6 servings

* If your food processor has a folding attachment or if you can use your whisk as one, use the manual control and slowly pour 3 tablespoons of egg whites into the salmon mixture and fold for 15 seconds. Stop the food processor. Pour the remaining egg whites into the soufflé mixture and, with the manual control, fold for about 1 minute.

CHEESE SOUFFLÉ WITH HAM
(SHREDDING BLADE; BLENDER OR STEEL BLADE; WHISK ATTACHMENT OR HAND BEATER)

This elegant soufflé, served in individual soufflé dishes, is a perfect start to an important dinner. For this soufflé to be a success, the egg whites must be very stiff and full of air. If your food processor does not have a whisk attachment, get out your electric beater or beat the whites by hand.

Ingredients

5 cups Béchamel Sauce (see page 182)

4 cups Cheddar cheese, cut into cubes

1 pound cooked ham, cubed

1 medium onion, quartered

Salt and pepper

4 tablespoons butter

¼ cup minced parsley

15 eggs, separated

Preheat the oven to 375°.

Remove the Béchamel Sauce from the heat. Grate the cheese and set aside.

Place the ham and onion, in batches, in the blender or work bowl and run the food processor for 1 minute until the onion is chopped.

In a heavy skillet, heat 2 tablespoons of butter. When the butter is hot, add the ham and onions. Sauté for 4 to 5 minutes until the onions are transparent. Add salt and pepper to taste.

Add the parsley to the skillet. Remove from heat, mix well, and set aside.

Pour the egg yolks into the blender or work bowl and beat for 2 seconds.

Add the beaten egg yolks to the Béchamel Sauce, stirring with a spoon until well mixed.

Cover the sauce and let cool for 20 minutes.

In the mixing bowl set with the whisk attachment, or using an electric or hand beater, beat the egg whites with a pinch of salt until they are very stiff.

Butter 6 small soufflé dishes with the remaining butter. Fold the Béchamel Sauce into the beaten egg whites using a wooden spoon, whisk or folding attachment:

- If folding with a wooden spoon, slowly pour one quarter of the egg whites into the Béchamel Sauce, folding gently so as not to break the whites. Then, slowly pour the Béchamel Sauce into the remaining egg whites, folding gently with a spoon.

- If using a whisk or folding attachment, pour the Béchamel Sauce into the mixing bowl. Using the manual control, pour in 3 tablespoons of egg whites and fold for 15 seconds. Pour in the remaining whites and fold for about 1 minute.

Fold 3½ cups of the grated cheese into the soufflé mixture:

- If using a wooden spoon, carefully fold 3½ cups of grated cheese into the soufflé mixture.
- If using a folding attachment, with the motor off, pour 3½ cups of grated cheese into the soufflé mixture. Turn on the manual control and fold for 10 seconds.

Reserve the remaining cheese.

Pour the soufflé mixture into the bottom third of the soufflé dishes. Cover with a layer of ham mixture. Pour the remaining soufflé mixture into each soufflé dish. Top with the reserved grated cheese.

Place the soufflé dishes on a baking sheet in a preheated 375° oven, and bake for 50 minutes.

When the soufflés are golden brown and cracked down the center, serve immediately.

Yield: 6 servings

STEAMED DUMPLINGS

This unusual dish, borrowed from the Chinese, makes an auspicious start to a lively meal. It is customary to place cruets on the table, one with hot oil, the other with white vinegar or soy sauce. Each diner pours several drops of vinegar or soy sauce onto his plate, adds a few drops of hot oil (see Note on page 56), and mixes the two with a hot dumpling. The dumpling dough may be prepared in the food processor or purchased at an Oriental food shop; it can be frozen.

The Dumpling Dough
(WHISK ATTACHMENT OR STEEL BLADE)

Ingredients

1 cup all-purpose flour   Pinch of salt
1 egg yolk   6 tablespoons water

In the mixing bowl or work bowl, add the flour, egg yolk, and salt. Mix for 3 seconds.

With the food processor running, add the water, tablespoon by tablespoon, to the dough; this will take approximately 10 seconds.

Yield: Dough for 20 dumplings

The Pork Filling
(BLENDER OR STEEL BLADE)

Ingredients

4 shrimp   3 water chestnuts, drained
½ cup cooked pork, cut into   1 egg
    1½-inch cubes   1 garlic clove
½ cup cooked chicken, cut   1 scallion, trimmed
    into 1½-inch cubes   Salt and pepper to taste

Plunge the shrimp into salted boiling water and cook for 6 minutes until pink. Drain and shell.

Place all the filling ingredients in the blender or work bowl. Run the food processor for 2 minutes, or until the mixture forms a thick paste.

To assemble the dumplings:

Roll the dough into a paper-thin rectangle.

Cut the dough into 2-inch squares.

Place 1 teaspoon of the meat mixture in the center of each square.

Fold each dough square in half to form a triangle. Press the edges firmly together. If the edges will not stick, moisten them with water and press.

When all the dumplings are filled and sealed, place them in a steamer, over boiling water, and steam them for 6 minutes. Drain and serve.

Note: Hot oil is available in Oriental food shops.

Yield: 20 dumplings

Cold Hors d'oeuvres

Two Pâtés

Pâtés taste far better after a few days in the refrigerator, which is fortunate since a pâté en gelée always takes two days to prepare. Despite the time allotment, pâtés are not all that difficult either to shop for or to prepare. And much of the time spent is waiting time. On the first day, after you have prepared your pâté and baked it in a bain marie, or pan of simmering water, it must sit overnight, weighted down so that the meat will be compressed and all the liquids squeezed out. On the second day, after you have made your aspic and cut out the decorations, you must wait, between steps, for the aspic to cool. Unless you make the aspic from scratch and clarify it, which we haven't the time for, there is very little to do that day. Pâtés are surprisingly gratifying to make and almost always well received.

FOUR-MEAT PÂTÉ
(MEAT GRINDER OR STEEL BLADE)

This highly seasoned pâté is made by placing layers of different types of meat on top of each other so that a lovely and colorful pattern emerges. At the center of each slice is a rosette of chicken liver, surrounded by pistachio nuts, olives, or, if you are feeling

[57]

flush, truffles. Four-meat pâté is not only delightful with drinks or as a first course, but as the high point of a light meal eaten indoors or out.

Since this pâté is made with individually seasoned meats, the proportions are not terribly important, and the pâté can be molded into many different shapes and prepared en gelée, en croûte, or both. You can feel free, too, to vary the ingredients, perhaps by adding ham or prosciutto or by replacing the chicken livers with hard-boiled eggs or deviled ham. If you are using a dry meat, such as veal, be sure to cover with a layer of fat so you will have a moist pâté.

The Pâté

Ingredients

1½ pounds veal, cut into 1½-inch cubes
1½ pounds fresh lean pork, cut into 1½-inch cubes
1½ pounds sweet Italian sausage
6 chicken livers
2 chicken breasts, skinned and boned
1 egg
½ teaspoon sage

3 shallots
3 tablespoons chopped parsley
Salt and pepper
½ cup cognac
3 tablespoons dried tarragon
Pistachio nuts, or olives, or truffles
½ pound fresh pork fat
2 slices fatback or bacon
Bay leaf (optional)

In this pâté each meat is seasoned separately. Before getting started, you would be wise to get out five bowls, one for each meat and one for the chicken livers.

Next, if not already on hand, chop the parsley and shallots, separately, in your blender or work bowl and set alongside the spices, cognac, and the egg.

Grind the veal in the meat grinder or in the work bowl for 2 minutes. Remove to a bowl.

Grind the pork in the meat grinder or in the work bowl for 2 minutes. Remove to a bowl.

Remove sausage meat from its casing by squeezing and place in a bowl.

Wash chicken livers well, removing any tendons. Cut in half and place in a bowl.

Skin and debone the chicken breasts. Reserve.

Prepare and season each meat separately, as follows:

To the ground veal, add the egg, ½ teaspoon of sage and 2 of the chopped shallots. Mix well.

To the ground pork, add 2 tablespoons of chopped parsley, the remaining chopped shallot, and salt and pepper. Mix well.

To the chicken livers, add 2 tablespoons of cognac, 3 tablespoons of tarragon, and salt and pepper. Stir.

Cut the chicken breasts into strips about ¾-inch wide. Place in a bowl and add the remaining cognac and the juice of the truffles, if used.

Cut the fresh pork fat into ¼-inch strips. Reserve.

Assemble the pâté:

Preheat the oven to 375°.

Place a slice of fatback or bacon in the bottom of a 1½-quart terrine or loaf pan. Spoon in half the sausage meat.

Lay the strips of chicken breast, lengthwise, over the sausage meat; spread the ground veal on top.

Next, place strips of pork fat on top of the veal, at quarter-inch intervals, parallel to the sides of the loaf pan.

Place the chicken livers in a row down the center of the pâté. Arrange the nuts, olives, or truffles around the chicken livers so that each slice will have some of their color (see illustration on page 60).

Spoon the ground fresh pork over the chicken-liver layer. Cover the pork layer with the remaining sausage meat.

Place a slice of fatback or bacon on top of the sausage. Top with a bay leaf.

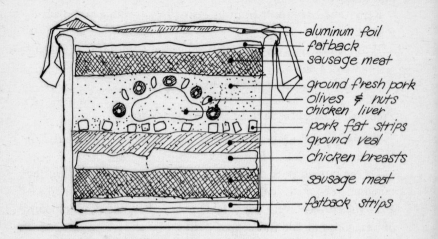

aluminum foil
fatback
sausage meat

ground fresh pork
olives & nuts
chicken liver

pork fat strips
ground veal
chicken breasts

sausage meat

fatback strips

Cover the pâté with the lid of the terrine or with aluminum foil; make a hole in the center for the steam to escape.

Bake the pâté in a bain marie, or pan of water, for 1½ hours at 375°.

When the pâté is cooked through, remove to a counter and weight with a brick or several 10-ounce cans so that the pâté will become dense. Let cool overnight before adding the aspic.

The Jellied Stock

Ingredients

3 cups beef or chicken stock or broth	Salt and pepper
2 envelopes unflavored gelatin	Olives, sliced carrots, fresh tarragon, or parsley for
1 teaspoon soy sauce	decoration

The following day, heat the broth or stock in a saucepan until it boils.

Meanwhile, in a bowl dissolve the gelatin in 2 tablespoons of cold water.

Add the gelatin to the broth and boil for 1 minute, stirring all the while. Add soy sauce for color, and salt and pepper to taste.

Remove to a bowl and let the broth cool to room temperature.

Meanwhile, pour all the liquid off the pâté and remove any unmelted bacon and the bay leaf.

Pour half of the cool but still liquid broth over the pâté and refrigerate for 15 minutes. Make decorations with olives and carrots and place them on the hardened aspic. When the design seems pleasing, cover with the remaining broth.

Refrigerate for at least one day, preferably two, before serving. Serve sliced, on a bed of lettuce, accompanied by Dijon or your favorite mustard.

Yield: 12 to 14 slices

Note: This pâté will still be good after a week to 10 days.

DUCK PÂTÉ
(BLENDER AND MEAT GRINDER OR STEEL BLADE)

This is a refined pâté to be served on a lettuce leaf, one slice per person, as the first course to a rather substantial meal. It is very rich indeed.

The Pâté

Ingredients

4½-pound duck
4 teaspoons salt
1½ teaspoons pepper
½ teaspoon tarragon
1 duck liver
3 chicken livers
½ pound lean pork, cut into
   1½-inch cubes
¼ pound duck fat

⅓ cup cognac
1 onion, quartered
1¼ cups heavy cream
2 eggs
3 tablespoons white wine
¼ teaspoon thyme
1½ teaspoons marjoram
6 slices pork fatback*

Preheat the oven to 325°.

Skin and bone the duck, or have your butcher do it for you.

Slice the breast into thin slices and place in a bowl. Add ½ teaspoon of salt and ¼ teaspoon of pepper. Sprinkle the breast meat with ½ teaspoon of tarragon and reserve.

Wash the chicken and duck livers well and remove the tendons. Pat dry.

Grind the rest of the duck meat, the pork, the duck fat, and the livers in your meat grinder, using the medium blade, or place, in batches, in the work bowl and run the food processor for 2 minutes, or until finely and evenly ground.

---

* If you cannot find fresh fatback, salted fatback will do. Be sure to blanch it first in boiling water for 5 minutes to remove the salt; drain and cut off the rind.

Remove the mixture to a bowl and add the cognac.

In the blender or work bowl, place the quartered onion, heavy cream, eggs, and white wine. Add the thyme and marjoram, and the remaining salt and pepper. Run the food processor for 30 seconds.

Add the ground meats and run the food processor for 10 seconds.

Line the bottom and the sides of a 1½-quart pâté mold or loaf pan with 3 slices of fatback.

Pour half the ground meat mixture into the pan and smooth the mixture.

Lay the duck breast slices, lengthwise, over the mixture.

Cover the layer of duck breast with the remaining ground meat mixture.

Place the remaining slices of fatback on top of the pâté.

Cover the pâté with the terrine lid or with aluminum foil; make a hole in the center of the foil so that steam can escape.

Place the pâté in a bain marie, or pan of water, in an oven preheated to 325°. Bake for 2 hours.

When you remove the pâté from the oven, weight it with a brick or two 10-ounce cans so that the pâté will become dense. Let stand overnight.

The Jellied Stock

Ingredients

3 cups duck, chicken, or beef
   broth or stock
1 tablespoon cognac or
   Madeira

2 envelopes unflavored gelatin
1 hard-boiled egg and parsley
   for decoration

The following morning, heat the stock or broth. Flavor it with cognac or Madeira.

In a small bowl, dissolve the gelatin in 2 tablespoons of cold water. Pour the gelatin into the broth and boil for 1 minute, stirring all the while. Reserve.

Uncover the pâté. Pour off any liquid and remove any remaining pieces of fatback from the top.

Pour half the broth over the pâté and place the pâté in the refrigerator for 15 minutes until the jellied stock has set slightly.

Make decorations with the hard-boiled egg and parsley and place on the gelatin. If necessary, use toothpicks to keep the decorations in place. (If you use toothpicks, remove them as soon as the new layer of jellied stock is slightly set; otherwise you will have holes in your aspic.)

Pour the remaining broth over the pâté. Cover and refrigerate for 24 hours before serving.

Slice and serve the pâté, one slice apiece, on a lettuce leaf.

Yield: 16 slices

RILLETTES
(BLENDER OR STEEL BLADE)

This flavorful pork paste is the pride of every French town and nearly every kitchen. Each cook believes he has found the most delicious blend of spices, and we are no exception. Rillettes, a favorite accompaniment to drinks, is usually served in earthenware crocks or terrines and spread on fresh, crusty white bread. Along with a vegetable or green salad, it makes a fine first course.

Ingredients

1 pound fresh pork fat, cut in 1½-inch cubes

1 pound lean pork, cut into 1½-inch cubes

1 tablespoon mixed spices (see page 29) or 1½ tablespoons marjoram or sage

2 teaspoons thyme

3 cups water

¼ pound fresh pork fat, sliced

1 teaspoon salt

1 teaspoon freshly ground pepper

In a heavy saucepan, melt half the pork fat until the cubes are crisp and brown. Remove the unmelted cubes with a slotted spoon and discard.

To the saucepan, add the pork, the remaining cubes of uncooked pork fat, the mixed spices, and the thyme. Add 3 cups of water and bring to a boil.

Reduce the heat and cook slowly for 2½ hours. If the water seems low, add half a cup more. Cook until the meat falls apart when pricked with a fork.

Pour the cooked meat into the blender or work bowl. Run the food processor for 2 minutes until the pork is a thick paste. Remove to a bowl.

Melt the slices of pork fat in a saucepan. Add 2 tablespoons of the melted fat to the bowl of pork paste and mix well. Add salt and pepper.

Taste and correct the seasonings; they should be spicy but not overpowering.

Spoon the rillettes into an earthenware terrine or any covered crockery. Refrigerate for at least a day before serving.

Yield: 1 quart

Note: Since rillettes keeps for at least a month and is no more difficult to prepare in large quantities, you may want to make several crockfuls at once. To preserve those that you plan to use last, melt extra pork fat in a saucepan and pour it over the cooling rillettes; the fat will harden and seal the meat. Refrigerate.

SHRIMP PÂTÉ WITH AVOCADO
(BLENDER OR STEEL BLADE)

This shrimp pâté, sliced and served with dressed avocado, is easy and elegant. Served uncut, the pâté is a delicacy to be spread on rounds of toasted bread.

The Pâté

Ingredients

1 pound shrimp	Salt and pepper to taste
1 stick butter, cut into 6 pieces	2 tablespoons cognac
¼ teaspoon cayenne	

Preheat the oven to 350°.

Wash the shrimp and plunge into 2 quarts of salted boiling water. Cook until the shrimp are pink, about 6 minutes.

Drain the shrimp, and when they are cool enough to handle, shell and devein. Cut the shrimp into 2 to 3 pieces.

Place the shrimp and butter in the blender or work bowl. Run the food processor for 2 minutes until the mixture forms a paste.

Add the cayenne, salt, and black pepper to taste. Add the cognac. Run the food processor for a fraction of a second, only to mix. Taste and correct the seasonings.

Grease a small loaf pan (approximately 4 x 6 inches) and pack the shrimp paste into the loaf pan.

Bake at 350° for 30 minutes.

When the top of the pâté is lightly browned, remove from the oven and let cool. Chill in the refrigerator overnight.

Serve sliced on individual plates, surrounded by avocado slices.

The Salad

Ingredients

2 medium avocados	¼ teaspoon salt
2 tablespoons oil	Pepper to taste
1½ tablespoons lemon juice	

Peel the avocados and slice.

In a bowl, mix the oil, lemon juice, salt, and pepper.

Pour sauce over the avocados and toss lightly.

Yield: 6 servings

HAM MOUSSE WITH
MORELS IN ASPIC
(BLENDER AND WHISK ATTACHMENT OR STEEL BLADE)

This mousse, pink shining through a pale gold aspic, will grace your
finest mold. It is a perfect dish for summertime, not only because
it is cool and light, but because it requires little actual cooking.
The mousse is quite delicate and spongy, with the dominant flavor
that of the pungent, almost peppery morels.

The Aspic

Ingredients

4 cups chicken stock or broth
¼ cup cognac
¼ teaspoon tarragon
2 envelopes unflavored gelatin

Salt and pepper to taste
Olives, carrots, and parsley for
  decoration

To make the aspic:

In a saucepan, bring the chicken stock or broth to a boil. Add the
cognac and tarragon, and continue boiling for 2 minutes.

Meanwhile, in a small bowl, dissolve the gelatin in 2 tablespoons
of cold water.

Add the gelatin to the broth and boil for 1 more minute, stirring
all the while with a wooden spoon. Add salt and pepper to taste.
Lower the flame and simmer, over low heat, for 10 minutes.

Strain the warm aspic through a very fine sieve or cheesecloth.

Let aspic stand at room temperature until it is cool.

To line the mold:

When the aspic is cool but still liquid, rinse a 6-cup mold in
cold water. Cover the bottom of the mold with a thin layer of aspic
and refrigerate for 10 minutes.

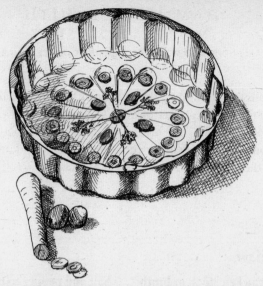

Cut the vegetables into decorative shapes and make a design on the hardened aspic (see illustration above).

Cover the vegetables with a layer of aspic and refrigerate for 10 more minutes.

When the bottom of the mold is well covered, pour on another layer of liquid aspic. This time, place the mold on its side in the refrigerator for 5 minutes. Repeat until the entire inside surface of the mold is covered with a thin layer of aspic.

The Mousse

Ingredients

2 ounces dried morels, soaked overnight in ½ cup water and milk (see Note, page 69)
3 tablespoons butter
Salt and pepper to taste
3 scallions, chopped

½ pound baked ham, cut into 1½-inch cubes
1 teaspoon tomato paste
½ teaspoon cayenne
½ cup heavy cream

Drain the morels and pat them dry. Place them in the blender or work bowl and run the food processor for 10 seconds.

[68]

Melt 3 tablespoons of the butter in a heavy skillet. When the butter is hot, sauté the morels for 3 minutes, until they are light brown. Sprinkle with salt and pepper. Set aside.

Without wiping out the blender or the work bowl, add the scallions, ham, tomato paste, and cayenne. Run the food processor for 2 minutes, or until the mixture becomes a puree.

Wash out the work bowl and add the heavy cream, or add the cream to your mixing bowl. Whip it lightly with the steel blade or whisk attachment until it is thick but not firm.

Using a rubber spatula or wooden spoon, fold the heavy cream into the ham puree.

Add ¾ cup of liquid aspic to the ham puree. Mix lightly.

Add the morels to the mousse and mix.

Spoon the mousse into the mold and refrigerate overnight.

To serve:

Unmold the mousse by dipping the mold quickly in a bowl of warm water. Place the mold on a round platter and tap the top with a knife; the mousse should slip right out. Surround the mousse with parsley sprigs and lemon wedges. Serve with a cold, dry white wine.

Yield: 10 servings

Note: If morels are unavailable, dried Chinese mushrooms can be substituted.

ZUCCHINI STUFFED WITH AVOCADO SALAD

(BLENDER OR STEEL BLADE)

Ingredients

6 medium zucchini, washed
  well
2 medium avocados, peeled
  and sliced
1 small onion
1 celery stalk, cut in pieces
¼ cup olive oil

1 tablespoon wine vinegar
1½ teaspoons salt
½ teaspoon pepper
6 fresh basil leaves or fresh
  mint leaves
3 hard-boiled eggs (optional)
  for decoration

Place the zucchini in a saucepan of boiling water and cook for 4 minutes. Drain.

When the zucchini are cool enough to handle, cut them in half lengthwise. Scoop out the pulp, taking care not to break the skins; the skins will be stuffed later on.

In the blender or work bowl, place the zucchini pulp and the avocados, onion, and celery. Run the food processor for a minute.

Add the olive oil, vinegar, and salt and pepper to the blender or work bowl. Run the food processor for 2 seconds to mix in the dressing. Taste and correct the seasonings.

Line up the zucchini shells and spoon the avocado salad into each one. Chill in the refrigerator for an hour.

Arrange the zucchini on a platter and garnish each with a leaf of basil or mint. Separate the stuffed zucchini with slices of hard-boiled eggs.

Yield: 6 servings

Note: These stuffed zucchini taste best served with hard salami or prosciutto.

BAY SCALLOP SALAD
(BLENDER OR STEEL BLADE; SLICING BLADE)

This salad is most pleasing when the scallops are barely cooked or, if you prefer, raw. Should you choose not to cook the scallops, marinate them in Vinaigrette for several hours. Serve in scallop shells and garnish with a sprig of parsley.

Ingredients

2 pounds bay scallops, washed
¼ cup lemon juice
½ cup Vinaigrette (see page 195)
1 cucumber
¼ cup large pitted green olives

3 celery stalks
1 cup mayonnaise (see page 177)
Salt and pepper to taste
6 scallop shells (optional)

Place the scallops in a saucepan, and cover with cold water. Add the lemon juice and bring to a boil; cook about 8 to 10 minutes, just until the scallops are firm when pierced with a fork.

Drain the scallops and place in a bowl. Cover with Vinaigrette. Toss the scallops in the dressing until mixed well. Set aside.

Peel and seed the cucumber and cut into several pieces. Place in the blender or work bowl and run the food processor for 10 seconds until the cucumber is practically a liquid. Remove to a bowl.

Set the slicing blade in place. Fit all the olives into the feed tube and push them through until they are sliced. Though some of the pieces will not be perfect, they will look fine when mixed in the salad.

Stand the celery stalks upright in the feed tube and push through to slice.

Add the celery and olives to the pureed cucumber. Add the mayonnaise, and mix well.

Spoon the cucumber dressing over the scallops. Toss. Add salt and pepper to taste.

When the salad is well mixed, chill it in the refrigerator for an hour.

To serve, spoon the salad into scallop shells or serve on a bed of watercress.

Yield: 6 first-course servings

STUFFED EGGS WITH ANCHOVIES AND NUTS
(BLENDER OR STEEL BLADE)

So that these stuffed eggs, sprinkled with pistachio nuts, stand upright it is a good idea to cut a thin slice off the bottom of each egg white. Removing the yolk from the hard-boiled egg without breaking the fragile white takes patience and understanding. We suggest cutting off the top third of the egg with a knife. Then when the egg is cool, hold the white in your hand, fingers wrapped around it, as though forming an egg cup, and dig out the yolk bit by bit with a demitasse spoon.

Ingredients

6 eggs
½ cup pistachio nuts
18 anchovy fillets
6 pickled onions
½ cup mayonnaise (see page 177)

½ teaspoon pepper
2 tomatoes, sliced (optional), for decoration
1 tablespoon chopped parsley (optional), for decoration

Before boiling the eggs, rub each one with a cut piece of lemon to prevent the shell from breaking. Then, place the eggs in boiling water and boil for 12 minutes. Remove eggs with a slotted spoon to a bowl of cold water. Let cool and shell.*

Meanwhile, shell the pistachio nuts. Blanch them in boiling water for 2 minutes to loosen the skin. Peel off the skin.*

Place the nuts in the blender or work bowl and run the food processor for 10 seconds until the nuts are finely chopped. Set aside.

When the eggs are cool, remove the yolks as described above. Cut off a slice of white from the bottom. Reserve unused cut portions of the whites for another use or discard.

Place the egg yolks in the blender or work bowl. Add 12 anchovy fillets and the pickled onions. Run the food processor for 40 seconds, or until the mixture forms a thick paste.

Add the mayonnaise and pepper to the mixture and run the food processor for 2 seconds.

Line up the egg whites and spoon the yolk mixture into the top until the effect is, once again, egg-shaped.

Sprinkle chopped pistachio nuts over the top of the filling.

Arrange the eggs on a platter, separating each with a tomato slice sprinkled with parsley.

Wrap an anchovy fillet around the base of each egg.

Yield: 6 servings

* The hard-boiled eggs and the pistachio nuts can be prepared the night before.

Four Vegetable Salads

In the spring and summertime, a table laden with a colorful array of vegetable salads is a glorious sight. These four are quite exquisite when served together with a pâté and cold cuts at luncheon or separately with a crepe as a first course.

ENDIVE AND BEET SALAD
(SLICING BLADE; BLENDER OR STEEL BLADE)

The beauty of this cold hors d'oeuvre lies in its colors. To keep the red of the beets from running over the endives, place the vegetables in separate layers in a serving bowl and toss lightly with your fingers. If you cannot find good endives, 4 or 5 sliced hard-boiled eggs will do nicely.

Ingredients

4 Belgian endives
10 medium beets, cooked, fresh
   or canned
⅓ cup heavy cream
2 scallions
1 teaspoon chopped parsley

1 teaspoon imported mustard,
   preferably Dijon
Juice of 1 lemon
Salt and pepper to taste
4 lettuce leaves, preferably
   Boston

Set the slicing blade in the food processor. Place the endives, two at a time, in the feed tube and slice them. Remove to a bowl.

Place the beets in the feed tube; cut them in half, if necessary, to fit. Run the food processor and repeat until all the beets are sliced. Remove the beets to a bowl.

Set the steel blade in the food processor. Pour the heavy cream into the blender or the work bowl, and beat the cream for 10 seconds. Reserve in a bowl.

Place the scallions in the blender or, after washing it, in the work bowl, and run the food processor for 3 seconds, until the scallions are minced. Set aside.

Add the chopped parsley, mustard, lemon juice, and salt and pepper, and run the food processor for 2 seconds, or until the ingredients are mixed well. Pour in the beaten cream and turn on the food processor for a fraction of a second, only to mix.

Place the lettuce leaves at the bottom of a serving bowl. Place a layer of endives on top. Next place a layer of beets and, on top of that, another layer of endives. Mix the salad lightly with your fingers.

Pour the cream dressing over the salad. Sprinkle minced scallion on top and serve.

Yield: 6 servings

CELERY RÉMOULADE
(JULIENNE OR SHREDDING BLADE; BLENDER OR STEEL BLADE)

Celery Rémoulade, to our palate, should have more than a hint of mustard. This one, with a touch of heavy cream, is very special; when mussels or shrimp are added, it is extraordinary.

Ingredients

1½ pounds celery root
2 tablespoons vinegar
1 tablespoon Dijon mustard
Juice of ½ lemon

2 tablespoons heavy cream
¼ cup mayonnaise (see page 177)
Salt and pepper to taste

Peel the celery root and cut into pieces to fit the feed tube.

Set the julienne or shredding blade in place. Fit the celery root pieces in the feed tube and push through. Repeat until all the celery root has been shredded.

In a large saucepan, set 2 quarts of water to boil. When the water is boiling, drop the celery root in. As soon as the water returns to a boil, drain. Immediately run the celery root under cold water to refresh it. Drain well.

Place the celery root in a bowl and add the vinegar. Refrigerate for 30 minutes.

If necessary, prepare the mayonnaise in your blender or work bowl. Add the mustard, lemon juice, and heavy cream to the mayonnaise and run the food processor for a fraction of a second to mix well.

Pour the dressing over the chilled celery root and mix well. Add salt and pepper to taste. Taste and correct the seasonings.

Refrigerate, covered, for an hour or more before serving.

Yield: 6 servings

Note: Celery Rémoulade can be stored, covered, in the refrigerator for several days.

ZUCCHINI SALAD
(BLENDER OR STEEL BLADE; SLICING BLADE)

Ingredients

1 medium onion, quartered	2 tablespoons lemon juice
2 pounds small zucchini	Salt and pepper to taste
6 tablespoons butter	2 sprigs fresh dill
3 tablespoons oil	Zucchini flowers (optional)*

Place the onion in the blender or work bowl and chop for 10 seconds.

Wash the zucchini and pat dry. Set the slicing blade in place. Fit the zucchini upright in the feed tube and push through to slice. Repeat until all the zucchini are sliced.

Melt the butter in a saucepan. Add the zucchini and the chopped onion to the saucepan and season with a pinch of salt and pepper to taste. Simmer, uncovered, for 20 minutes, or until the zucchini are barely tender. Remove with a slotted spoon to a serving bowl.

---

* Zucchini flowers are quite common in summer vegetable gardens. If you find some, boil them for a few seconds, drain, and add to the salad.

In a small bowl, or in the blender or work bowl, add the oil, lemon juice, and salt and pepper to taste. Mix well.

Pour the dressing over the zucchini. Snip the dill over the top. Toss the salad lightly and refrigerate, covered, for an hour.

Yield: 6 servings

CUCUMBER SALAD WITH YOGURT
(SLICING BLADE; BLENDER OR STEEL BLADE)

Cucumber salad, an easy, informal hors d'oeuvre when served with olives and cold meats, is especially welcome before charcoal-broiled meat or any lamb dish. Its ability to cool the palate after a spicy dish is known to many cultures.

Ingredients

2 medium cucumbers, peeled
1 tablespoon salt
2 cups yogurt
1 garlic clove
1 teaspoon dill, fresh if possible

1 tablespoon mint, fresh if possible
2 tablespoons lemon juice
2 tablespoons olive oil
Salt and pepper to taste

Set the slicing blade in place. Stand the cucumbers upright in the feed tube and push through to slice. If a cucumber is too wide for the feed tube, shave off one side or, if necessary, slice the cucumber in half.

Place the sliced cucumbers in a bowl and sprinkle with the salt to help force the liquid out. Let stand for 15 minutes.

In the blender or work bowl, place the yogurt, garlic, dill, mint, and lemon juice, and run the food processor for 20 seconds. Add the olive oil and salt and pepper to taste. Run the food processor for 2 seconds to mix.

Pour the liquid off the cucumbers; the cucumbers should be quite crisp.

Add the yogurt mixture to the cucumbers and chill.

Yield: 4 to 6 servings

Seasoned Butters for Crudités

CRUDITÉS

One of the simplest and most appealing companions to drinks, any time of day, is crudités, or raw vegetables. Look for fresh, unblemished vegetables in season. Choose those that are easy to hold in the hand. And select an assortment that will please and surprise the eye.

Ingredients

4 carrots, cut in sticks
½ pound string beans
1 head cauliflower, broken into
    flowerets and reassembled

3 green peppers, seeded and
    cut in strips
6 scallions
1 bunch fresh radishes, bearded
    but with leaves left on

The vegetables can be washed, chilled, and, when called for, scraped and sliced ahead of time. Arrange the crudités in straw baskets and serve with any of the following seasoned butters.

SEASONED BUTTERS

These butters may be served alone or in pairs. In addition to being the perfect complement to crudités, they can be used in many other ways. A curl of seasoned butter, lightly chilled, is splendid as it melts over a small broiled steak. Any of these butters is delicious stuffed into mushroom caps or cherry tomatoes to be eaten raw or broiled. Here are four offerings; the variations are endless. For ease in preparing, take the butter out of the refrigerator 20 minutes ahead of time.

Butter Seasoned with Blue Cheese
(BLENDER OR STEEL OR PLASTIC BLADE)

Ingredients

1 stick butter, cut in 6 pieces   ¼ pound blue cheese, cut in cubes

In the blender or work bowl, place the butter and the blue cheese. Run the food processor for 20 seconds, or until the butter forms a thick paste. Remove to a serving bowl or ramekin.

Marrow Butter
(BLENDER OR STEEL BLADE)

Ingredients

4 beef marrow bones
4 shallots
½ cup white wine

1 stick butter, cut in 10 to 12 pieces
1 tablespoon chopped parsley
Salt and pepper to taste

Wash the marrow bones under cold running water. Place the bones in a saucepan and cover with water; bring to a boil. Simmer for 10 minutes. Drain.

When the marrow bones are cool enough to handle, remove the marrow from each by tapping the bone on a counter top or by scraping along the inside of the bone with a paring knife. Chill the marrow in the refrigerator.

Meanwhile, in the blender or work bowl, chop the shallots and set aside.

Pour the white wine in a saucepan and bring to a boil. Add the chopped shallots and simmer for 10 minutes, or until the liquid is reduced by half.

Pour the reduced wine mixture into the blender or work bowl. Cut the butter into small pieces and retrieve the chilled marrow.

With the food processor running, drop the butter, a few pieces at a time, through the feed tube; this will take approximately 10 seconds. Stop the motor.

Start the food processor and drop the marrow through the feed tube; let the food processor continue running for 15 seconds, or until the butter is creamed. Add the chopped parsley and salt and pepper to taste. Run the food processor for a fraction of a second until the butter is well mixed. Remove to a bowl or ramekin.

Herbal Butter
(BLENDER OR STEEL BLADE)

The quantity of herbs suggested here is fairly standard, but the selection can vary depending on what fresh herbs are available. Butters can be made with a single herb, such as dill or tarragon. Parsley goes with almost any herb.

Ingredients

2 sprigs watercress
2 sprigs parsley
4 or 5 basil leaves

1–2 sticks butter, cut in small
  pieces
Salt and pepper to taste

Add the fresh herbs to the blender or work bowl. Run the food processor for 15 seconds.

Start the food processor again, and drop the butter, a few pieces at a time, through the feed tube until you have added one stick. Taste. If the herbs seem too powerful, start the food processor and add a few more pieces of butter. Stop the machine and taste again. Repeat until the herbal butter pleases you. Season with salt and pepper, and remove to a bowl or ramekin.

Butter Seasoned with Horseradish
(SHREDDING BLADE; BLENDER OR STEEL BLADE)

Ingredients

2-inch piece fresh horseradish, if possible, or 2 tablespoons bottled

1 stick butter, cut in 6 pieces

Set the food processor with the medium shredding blade. Cut a 2-inch slice of horseradish and place in the feed tube. Push through to grate.

Place the horseradish and the butter in the blender or work bowl. Run the food processor for 20 seconds until the butter is smooth.

Remove to a small bowl or ramekin.

Soups

Two Basic Stocks

CHICKEN STOCK

Ingredients

2 marrow bones
1 4-pound fowl or 4 pounds of chicken backs and giblets
4 quarts water
2 tablespoons salt
5 peppercorns
3 carrots
2 celery stalks

3 leeks (optional)
1 medium onion stuck with 2 cloves
4 sprigs parsley
1 sprig of fresh thyme, or ½ teaspoon dried thyme
1 small bay leaf

Under cold running water, rinse off the marrow bones and wash the fowl or chicken backs and giblets.

Place the fowl and marrow bones in a heavy kettle. Cover with 4 quarts of water and bring slowly to a full boil, skimming the froth from the top as it rises. Reduce the heat and add the salt and peppercorns. Simmer for an hour.

Scrape the carrots; wash and trim the celery, and cut into 2 or 3 pieces. Wash the leeks well and trim. Add the carrots, celery, leeks, and the onion stuck with cloves to the stock. Add the herbs, tied with string or in cheesecloth, and continue simmering for 1½ hours more.

When the stock has simmered for 2½ hours, strain through a very fine sieve covered with cheesecloth or through two layers of cheesecloth. Discard the bones and vegetables, and reserve the fowl for another use.*

Let the stock cool to room temperature, then refrigerate for several hours or overnight.

The following morning, remove the congealed fat from the top and reheat the stock slowly. Pour into 1- or 1½-quart containers. Freeze any stock you do not plan to use within the next few days.

Yield: About 3 quarts

* For dishes prepared with stewed chicken or fowl, see the section on leftovers.

BEEF STOCK

Ingredients

1½ pounds beef shins
1½ pounds beef marrow bones
3 tablespoons oil
4 quarts water
2 tablespoons salt
4–6 black peppercorns
2 celery stalks

2 carrots
2 onions stuck with a clove
  apiece
2 sprigs fresh thyme, or 1
  teaspoon dried thyme
3 sprigs parsley

Under cold running water, wash the beef shins and rinse off the marrow bones.

Heat the oil in a heavy kettle and, when it is hot, add the beef shins. Sauté for a few minutes to brown.

Add the marrow bones to the kettle and cover with 4 quarts of water. Bring slowly to a full boil, skimming the froth from the top as it rises. Reduce the heat, add the salt and peppercorns, and simmer for an hour.

Wash and trim the celery and cut into several large pieces; scrape the carrots. Add these and the onions stuck with cloves to the soup.

Tie the herbs together with a string or, if using loose thyme, with cheesecloth, and add.

Bring the soup to a second boil, lower the flame, and simmer for 2 hours.

When the stock is cooked, let it cool to room temperature before refrigerating for several hours or overnight.

The following morning, remove the congealed fat from the top and reheat the stock slowly. Strain through a sieve or a layer of cheesecloth and, unless you are making a heavy beef soup, discard the meat and vegetables; they will have given up most of their flavor.

Pour the stock into 1- or 1½-quart plastic containers and freeze for future use. The stock will keep in the refrigerator for 3 or 4 days.

Yield: Just under 3 quarts

ONION SOUP GRATINÉE
(SLICING BLADE; SHREDDING BLADE)

This soup, its broth rich with butter and onions, is covered with a thick crust of melted Gruyère. It is welcome, all winter long, before a light supper or a fairly full meal.

Ingredients

½ pound yellow onions
6 tablespoons butter
2 tablespoons flour
2 quarts beef or chicken stock
  or broth

Salt and pepper to taste
1¼ pounds Gruyère cheese
6 slices French or Italian bread

Preheat the oven to 200°.

Peel and halve the onions. Set the slicing blade in place, fit the onions in the feed tube, and push through until all are sliced.

In a large skillet, melt 3 tablespoons of butter. Add the onions and sauté them over a low flame until they are transparent. Sprinkle flour over the onions and stir until they are coated.

Add the chicken or beef stock to the skillet and bring quickly to a boil. Lower the flame and simmer for 25 minutes, stirring occasionally. Season with salt and pepper to taste.

Meanwhile, cut the Gruyère into pieces to fit the feed tube, and set aside 4 ounces to be grated. Fit the rest of the Gruyère in the feed tube and push through until the cheese is sliced thin.

Set the shredding blade in place and fit the reserved Gruyère in the feed tube. Push through until you have approximately 1 cup of grated cheese.

In a 200° oven, dry out the French bread for 10 minutes. Remove the bread and turn oven heat to 400°.

After 25 minutes, when the soup is cooked, taste and correct the seasonings. Line up individual bowls, preferably gratinée bowls, and spoon the soup in, dividing the onions among them.

Add 2 tablespoons of grated Gruyère to each bowl and mix. Float a piece of bread on top. Cover the bread with 3 or 4 thin slices of Gruyère, arranging the cheese so that when it is baked it will form a crust over the soup. Cut the remaining butter into small pieces and place a pat on top of the cheese.

Just before serving time, place the bowls in the preheated 400° oven and bake until the cheese is golden brown and toasty. Serve the soup steaming hot.

Yield: 6 servings

CREAM OF MUSHROOM SOUP
(BLENDER OR STEEL BLADE)

This rich mushroom soup, with a touch of sherry, is a very fine one. Be sure to garnish it with a sprinkling of parsley and, if you can find them, firm white mushroom caps.

Ingredients

1 pound mushrooms
4 tablespoons butter
¼ cup flour
¼ teaspoon pepper
4 cups chicken broth
1 cup heavy cream

¼ cup dry sherry
Salt and pepper to taste
6 medium, white, firm mushroom caps for garnish
Chopped parsley for garnish

Wash the mushrooms and dry well. Place the mushrooms in the blender or work bowl and run the food processor for 10 seconds, or until finely chopped.

In a large saucepan, melt the butter. When it is hot, add the mushrooms and cover. Cook over a medium heat, stirring occasionally, for 5 minutes.

Uncover the mushrooms and, stirring constantly with a wooden spoon, add the flour and pepper. When the mushrooms are coated, lower the flame and continue to stir for 3 more minutes. Little by little, add the chicken broth to the saucepan. Stir occasionally until the broth is heated through.

Then, taking care not to let the broth boil, slowly stir the cream in. When the cream is incorporated, stir in the sherry, and add salt and pepper to taste. Remove from the heat and correct the seasonings.

Wash the 6 mushroom caps and place one in each bowl. At serving time, reheat the soup and spoon it over the mushroom caps, hollow side down. Sprinkle with chopped parsley and serve at once.

Yield: 6 servings

CREAM OF SPINACH SOUP
(SHREDDING BLADE)

This simple cream soup is at its finest when the spinach is cooked quickly so that it retains its freshness. The garniture, croutons with a hint of bacon, is a master stroke.

Ingredients

1 pound spinach	Salt and pepper to taste
5 tablespoons butter	1 cup heavy cream
¼ cup flour	Croutons for garnish (see
4 cups chicken stock or broth	page 91)

Wash the spinach well and trim it; pat dry. Set the shredding blade in place and drop the spinach, a few leaves at a time, into the feed tube. Push through until all the spinach is shredded into thin ribbons, or chiffonades.

Over a low flame, melt the butter in a saucepan. Blend in the flour with a wooden spoon, and stir for 2 or 3 minutes until the roux is mixed well.

Gradually add the chicken stock to the saucepan and cook, stirring constantly, for 5 minutes.

Add the shredded spinach to the stock and season with salt and pepper to taste.

Heat the soup just under the boiling point and slowly stir in the cream. Correct the seasonings and remove from heat.

Serve in a soup tureen, accompanied by croutons.

Yield: 6 servings

CROUTONS

Ingredients

4 slices stale white bread,
  crusts removed
2 slices bacon or 1 tablespoon
  bacon fat

4 tablespoons butter
1 tablespoon minced parsley

Cut the bread into half-inch cubes.

Unless you have bacon fat on hand, cook 2 pieces of bacon in a skillet, reserving the bacon and all but 1 tablespoon of the fat for another use.

Heat the butter and bacon fat in the skillet and, when it is hot, add the cubed bread. Sauté, stirring frequently, over high heat until the croutons are golden brown.

With a slotted spoon, transfer the croutons to paper towels to soak up the oils; pat with paper towels to dry.

Place the toasted croutons in a bowl, sprinkle with minced parsley, and serve alongside the soup.

CREAM OF BROCCOLI
(BLENDER OR STEEL BLADE)

Ingredients

2 pounds broccoli
8 cups chicken broth or stock
1 large bay leaf
2 sprigs parsley
1 sprig thyme, or 1 teaspoon
  dried thyme

2 tablespoons butter
2 tablespoons flour
Salt and pepper to taste
2 egg yolks
1 cup heavy cream
½ teaspoon grated nutmeg

Wash and trim the broccoli and set aside 6 small flowerets for garnish. Cut the broccoli flowers and stalks into pieces that will cook evenly and place in a large saucepan. Cover with the chicken stock or broth.

Add the herbs, tied with a string or in cheesecloth, to the saucepan, and bring the stock to a boil. Lower the flame and cook, covered, for 35 minutes, until the broccoli is tender but not falling apart.

Pour the soup through a colander or strainer into a bowl. Discard the herbs and place the broccoli and 3 tablespoons of soup into the blender or work bowl. Run the food processor for 30 seconds until the broccoli is pureed.

Melt the butter in a saucepan over a low heat. Add the flour, and stir for 2 or 3 minutes to make a roux. Little by little, stir in the reserved chicken stock; bring to a boil.

Bring the stock to a boil and add the pureed broccoli. Season with salt and pepper to taste. Turn the flame down very low.*

Place the egg yolks and heavy cream in the blender or work bowl and run the food processor for 3 seconds to mix. Add 2 tablespoons of stock to the mixture to warm it before adding it to the hot soup.

Now, stirring constantly with a wooden spoon, slowly add the beaten eggs and cream to the soup.

Before serving, reheat the soup so that it thickens slightly, but do not let it boil. Spoon the soup into individual bowls, sprinkle with grated nutmeg, and garnish with broccoli flowerets.

Yield: 6 servings

* The soup may be made several hours ahead to this point.

CARROT AND LEEK SOUP
(SLICING BLADE; BLENDER OR STEEL BLADE)

Ingredients

1½ pounds carrots
5 leeks
5 sprigs parsley
1 large bay leaf

6 cups chicken stock or broth
Salt and pepper to taste
½ cup heavy cream
3 tablespoons butter
Chopped parsley for garnish

Scrape the carrots. Wash the leeks well to get out all the sand, and trim.

Set the slicing blade in place and fit the carrots and leeks upright in the feed tube; push through until all are sliced.

Place the carrots, leeks, parsley sprigs, and bay leaf in a saucepan. Add water to cover and bring to a boil; lower the flame and simmer for 20 minutes until the vegetables are tender.

With a slotted spoon, transfer the carrots and leeks to the blender or work bowl. Add ½ cup of the cooking liquid and run the food processor for 2 minutes, or until the vegetables are pureed.

In a saucepan, heat the chicken stock. Add the pureed vegetables to the hot stock and stir. Add salt and pepper to taste. Continue to cook the soup just until the vegetables are heated through.

Lower the flame and slowly stir in the heavy cream, taking care not to let the soup boil. Before serving, swirl in the butter. Serve the soup in a tureen and garnish with chopped parsley.

Yield: 6 servings

WATERCRESS SOUP
(BLENDER OR STEEL BLADE)

Ingredients

3 large boiling potatoes
1 large onion
6 cups chicken stock or broth
2 bunches watercress

Salt and pepper to taste
3 egg yolks
½ cup heavy cream

Peel and quarter the potatoes and onion. Place them in a sauce-pan, cover with the chicken stock or broth, and bring to a boil. Lower the flame and simmer for 20 minutes, until the potatoes are tender when pierced with a fork.

Wash and trim the watercress and dry well. Place in the blender or work bowl and run the food processor for 20 seconds to chop; set aside.

When the potatoes and onion are cooked, transfer them with a slotted spoon to the blender or work bowl. Add 3 tablespoons of chicken stock and run the food processor for 15 seconds to puree.

Spoon the potato-and-onion puree into a heavy kettle. Add the chopped watercress, and pour the chicken stock from the saucepan over the vegetables. Bring the soup to a boil, stirring constantly with a wooden spoon, and add salt and pepper to taste. Reduce the flame to a very low light.

Place the egg yolks in the blender or work bowl and, with the food processor running, pour the heavy cream through the feed tube in a steady stream; continue running the motor for 30 seconds until the eggs and cream are very well mixed.

Stirring all the while, slowly add the beaten eggs and cream to the soup. Heat the soup for 3 to 4 minutes to thicken it slightly, but do not let it boil or the eggs will scramble. When the soup reaches the desired consistency, remove from the flame and serve immediately.

Yield: 6 servings

ROMAINE AND MARROW SOUP
(BLENDER OR STEEL BLADE)

The delicate puffs of marrow transform this easy and inexpensive soup into a dish that is beautiful and refined.

Ingredients

4 beef marrow bones
8 large romaine lettuce leaves
6 cups chicken stock or broth

Salt and pepper to taste
1 tablespoon butter

Wash the marrow bones under cold running water and place in a kettle. Cover with water and bring to a boil; reduce heat and simmer for 10 minutes. Drain the bones and chill in the refrigerator for about 45 minutes until the marrow has solidified so that it can be sliced with ease.

Meanwhile, wash and dry the outer leaves of a head of romaine, reserving the tender inner leaves for salad. Place the leaves in the blender or work bowl and run the food processor for 15 seconds until the romaine is finely chopped.

Pour the chicken stock or broth in the kettle and heat. When the soup is quite hot but not boiling, add the romaine. Season with salt and pepper to taste, and continue to cook while preparing the marrow.

Retrieve the chilled bones and remove the marrow, either by scraping around the inside rim with a knife or by tapping the bones on a counter top. Cut the marrow into ½-inch thick slices and add to the stock. Turn off the flame.

At serving time, add the butter and reheat the soup. Serve at once with French or Italian bread.

Yield: 6 servings

ZUCCHINI AND FRESH PEA SOUP
(BLENDER OR STEEL BLADE)

This extremely light soup is best in the spring and summertime when the zucchini are small and the peas very crisp. Should you choose to serve this soup cold, add sour cream and mix well before chilling for several hours.

Ingredients

5 small zucchini
1 onion, quartered
1 cup fresh peas
6 cups chicken stock or broth
1 teaspoon oregano

Salt and pepper to taste
6 tablespoons sour cream
  (optional)
6 fresh basil leaves or mint
  leaves

Wash the zucchini. Cut into 3 or 4 pieces and place in a saucepan.

Add the onion, peas, and chicken broth and bring to a boil. Lower the flame and season with oregano and salt and pepper to taste. Simmer for 20 minutes.

Transfer the peas, zucchini, and onion with a slotted spoon to the blender or work bowl. Add ½ cup of broth and run the food processor for 15 seconds, or until the vegetables are pureed.

Return the puree to the saucepan and mix well. Heat through before serving and correct the seasonings.

Spoon the soup into individual bowls, top with sour cream and a fresh basil or mint leaf.

Yield: 6 servings

GRANDMOTHER'S SOUP
(SLICING BLADE; SHREDDING BLADE)

This wonderfully subtle vegetable soup tastes mainly of celery root and leeks. It is a wholesome soup, nonetheless, especially good before pasta or meat and potatoes.

Ingredients

2 boiling potatoes, peeled
1 pound celery root, peeled
3 carrots, scraped
3 medium leeks, washed and
   trimmed
3 celery stalks, trimmed
3 endives
4 tablespoons butter
4 cups chicken or beef stock
   or broth

Salt and pepper to taste
1¾ cups milk
½ cup heavy cream
2 ounces Gruyère cheese, or
   ½ cup grated
6 slices of French or Italian
   bread
Parsley sprigs for garnish
   (optional)

Set the slicing blade in place and fit the potatoes in the feed tube. Push through to slice. Reserve.

Cut all the other vegetables into pieces that will fit the feed tube of the food processor. Fit them in the feed tube, in whatever order and combination you choose, and push through until all are sliced.

Melt the butter in a heavy kettle. Add all the vegetables, except the potatoes, to the kettle and cook gently, covered, for 20 minutes.

To the kettle add the sliced potatoes, the chicken or beef stock, and salt and pepper to taste. Bring the soup to a boil, reduce heat, and simmer.

After 30 minutes, add the milk and cream, taking care not to let them boil. Continue simmering the soup for 15 more minutes.

Meanwhile, grate the Gruyère, using the shredding blade.

Near serving time, place the bread on a broiler pan and cover each slice with Gruyère. Set the bread under the broiler until the cheese is toasted and golden.

Spoon the cooked soup into individual bowls, top with toasted bread, and garnish with a sprig of parsley.

Yield: 6 servings

GARLIC SOUP WITH ALMONDS
(BLENDER OR STEEL BLADES)

This piquant winter soup should be started early in the day, or even a day ahead. Use plenty of pepper and sufficient garlic to flavor the soup without overpowering it.

Ingredients

1 lean ham bone with at least a quarter pound of meat left on

6 cups chicken stock or broth, or water

6 parsley sprigs

1 bay leaf

¼ teaspoon thyme

18 almonds, shelled

¼ cup olive oil

6 slices French or Italian bread

3 garlic cloves

Salt and pepper to taste

Chopped parsley for garnish

In a large saucepan, cover the ham bone with the chicken stock or water and bring to a boil. Add the parsley, bay leaf, and thyme, and boil the soup for 1 hour, or until the meat falls off the ham bone.

Discard the ham bone and remove the meat from the soup with a slotted spoon. Reserve the meat.

Place the soup in the refrigerator and cool for 3 hours or overnight.

Meanwhile, blanch the almonds in boiling water for 3 minutes to remove the skin. Drain and pat dry.

Heat the olive oil in a heavy skillet and, when it is hot, add the almonds and the bread. Sauté the almonds and the bread for several minutes until they are golden brown.

In the blender or work bowl, place the garlic cloves, the reserved ham, and the bread and almonds. Run the food processor for 1 minute, or until all the ingredients are pureed.

Retrieve the soup from the refrigerator and skim off the hardened fat.

Add the garlic-and-almond puree to the soup and stir. Bring the soup to a boil, lower the heat, and simmer for 20 minutes. Add salt and pepper to taste and correct the seasonings; it should be quite peppery. Garnish with chopped parsley and serve hot.

Yield: 6 servings

MOREL BISQUE WITH SPINACH
(BLENDER OR STEEL BLADE)

This elegant bisque calls for only a bit of each ingredient. Prepare it quickly, at the last minute, and you will have a fresh and delicate treat.

Ingredients

6 ounces dry morels soaked
    overnight in ½ cup milk
1 cup parsley, tightly packed
1½ cups fresh spinach
2 scallions, trimmed
2 tablespoons butter
½ cup dry white wine

Salt and pepper to taste
1 quart chicken stock or broth
2 egg yolks
1 cup heavy cream
1 lemon, sliced thin, for garnish
Paprika

Drain the morels and pat dry with paper towels.
Wash the scallions, parsley, and spinach, and dry well.

Place the morels in the blender or work bowl and run the food processor for 10 seconds. Remove the finely chopped morels to a bowl.

Add the parsley to the blender or work bowl and run the food processor for 5 seconds. Add the spinach and scallions and run the food processor for 5 more seconds, or until chopped fine.

Melt the butter in a large saucepan. When the butter is hot, add the morels and sauté them gently for 3 minutes until they are a light brown. Add the parsley, spinach, and scallions, and simmer for 2 minutes.

To the saucepan, add the wine and salt and pepper to taste. Pour in the chicken broth or stock, bring to a boil, reduce heat, and simmer the soup for 10 minutes.

Meanwhile, add the egg yolks and the heavy cream to the blender or work bowl and run the food processor for 3 seconds to mix.

Pour the beaten eggs and cream in a slow stream into the soup, stirring constantly with a wooden spoon and taking care not to let the soup boil. When all the cream is incorporated, remove the saucepan from the heat.

Serve the morel bisque in individual bowls. Float a slice of lemon on top and sprinkle each slice with paprika.

Yield: 6 servings

COLD TOMATO AND BASIL SOUP
(SLICING BLADE; BLENDER OR STEEL BLADE)

Ingredients

6 ripe medium tomatoes
3 medium onions
½ cup olive oil
2 garlic cloves, quartered
1 teaspoon sugar
1 teaspoon salt
1 tablespoon tomato paste

12–15 basil leaves
2 tablespoons flour, preferably
  potato flour
4 cups chicken broth
1 cup water (optional)
Salt and pepper to taste
6 basil leaves for garnish

Wash the tomatoes and halve them. Halve the onions.

Set the slicing blade in place and fit the tomatoes and onions into the feed tube. Push through until all the onions and tomatoes are sliced; they will be pureed later on.

Pour half the olive oil into a saucepan and heat. When the oil is hot, add the tomatoes, onions, garlic, sugar, 1 teaspoon of salt, and tomato paste. When the liquid is boiling, lower the heat, and let simmer for 20 minutes.

Place the basil leaves in the blender or work bowl and run the food processor for 5 seconds to chop. Set aside.

Place the flour in the blender or work bowl and moisten with a few drops of chicken broth. With the food processor running, slowly pour 1 cup of chicken broth through the feed tube until the mixture is a thick paste. Pour the remaining broth through the feed tube at a moderate pace until the soup is thoroughly mixed.*

When the tomatoes and onions are limp, add the broth to the saucepan. If necessary, thin the soup with a cup of water. Add the chopped basil leaves and stir. Cook for 4 minutes.

Pour half the soup into the blender or work bowl and run for 2

---

* If using a work bowl, after adding 2 cups of broth, remove mixture to a bowl. Pour the remaining chicken broth into the bowl and mix well.

minutes until pureed. Remove to a bowl. Repeat, adding the remaining olive oil. Combine and mix well with a wooden spoon. Season with salt and pepper to taste.

Refrigerate for at least 2 hours.

Serve in chilled bowls and garnish with a fresh basil leaf.

Yield: 6 servings

CUCUMBER AND STRING BEAN SOUP
(BLENDER OR STEEL BLADE)

This soup, which takes only a matter of minutes, inspires variation. Instead of string beans, you can combine cucumbers with lima beans, cooked asparagus, or ripe avocado.

Ingredients

½ pound string beans	4 cups yogurt
4 cucumbers	Salt and pepper to taste
2 garlic cloves	3 sprigs dill

Drop the beans into 1½ quarts salted boiling water and cook for 6 or 7 minutes until tender. Drain.

Meanwhile, peel the cucumbers and cut each into 5 or 6 pieces. Place the cucumbers, string beans, and garlic cloves in the blender or work bowl and run the food processor until the vegetables are pureed.

With the food processor running, pour the yogurt through the feed tube in a steady stream; this will take about 1 minute.

Pour the soup into a bowl, and add salt and pepper to taste.

Refrigerate for an hour or two. At serving time, snip the dill and sprinkle on top.

Yield: 6 servings

COLD CUCUMBER AND BEET SOUP

(SHREDDING BLADE; BLENDER OR STEEL BLADE)

Ingredients

2 medium cucumbers
1 pound cooked beets, fresh
  or canned
1 small onion, halved
1 tablespoon chopped parsley

6 cups chicken broth
Salt and pepper to taste
6 tablespoons sour cream
3 sprigs dill, chopped

Peel the cucumbers, cut lengthwise, and remove the seeds with a spoon. Cut into pieces to fit the feed tube.

Drain the beets, and cut in half.

Set the shredding blade in place. Fit the cucumbers and beets in the feed tube and push through. Remove to a bowl.

Place the onion in the blender or work bowl and chop for 5 seconds. Add to the bowl.

Add the chopped parsley to the beets, cucumbers, and onions.

In a saucepan, heat the chicken broth. When the soup is hot, pour it over the shredded beets and cucumbers and mix well. Add salt and pepper to taste.

Chill the soup for 2 hours. Serve cucumber and beet soup in individual bowls. Top each serving with 1 tablespoon of sour cream and sprinkle with chopped dill.

Yield: 6 servings

COLD SORREL SOUP
(BLENDER OR STEEL BLADE)

This rich soup is splendid cold. Should you choose to serve it hot, instead of chopping the sorrel fine, shred it, using the shredding blade, into thin ribbons or chiffonades. As soon as the soup has thickened, swirl in a pat of butter and serve at once.

Ingredients

2 medium boiling potatoes
4 cups chicken stock or broth
1 pound sorrel
4 egg yolks

1 cup light cream
Salt and pepper to taste
Grated nutmeg (optional)

Wash and peel the potatoes. Quarter them so that they will cook quickly.

Place the potatoes in a saucepan and cover with the chicken stock or broth. Bring the stock to a boil and simmer until the potatoes are tender when pierced with a fork.

Meanwhile, wash the sorrel and cut off the stems. Place in the blender or work bowl and run the food processor for 1 minute until the sorrel is finely chopped. Set aside.

When the potatoes are cooked, remove them from the stock with a slotted spoon and place in the blender or work bowl. Run the food processor until the potatoes are pureed. Return the potatoes to the chicken stock and stir until mixed well.

Add the sorrel to the soup and simmer for 5 minutes.

Add the egg yolks to the blender or work bowl and run the food processor for 2 seconds. Then, with the motor running, slowly pour in the light cream and beat until the mixture is frothy. Add 2 tablespoons of the soup to the egg-and-cream mixture.

Gradually add the beaten eggs and cream to the soup and let simmer for 5 minutes, stirring all the while. Season with salt and pepper to taste.

Pour the soup into a serving bowl and chill in the refrigerator for several hours. Sprinkle with grated nutmeg before serving.

Yield: 6 servings

COLD CELERY AND POTATO SOUP
(SLICING BLADE; BLENDER OR STEEL BLADE)

Ingredients

3 large boiling potatoes
5 cups chicken stock or broth
1 teaspoon salt
½ teaspoon dried tarragon
½ teaspoon fresh savory, or
 ¼ teaspoon dried savory

6 celery stalks
1 large onion
2 tablespoons butter
½ cup light cream
6 radishes, sliced, for garnish

Peel and quarter the potatoes. Place in a saucepan with the chicken stock or broth, salt, tarragon, and savory. Cook over a low flame for about 15 minutes until the potatoes are tender when pierced with a fork.

Meanwhile, wash and trim the celery. Set the slicing blade in place. Fit the celery and the onion in the feed tube and push through to slice.

In a large saucepan, melt the butter. Add the celery and onions and cook over a low flame, stirring occasionally, for 10 minutes, until the onion is transparent.

Add the onion and celery to the broth.

Puree the soup in batches in the blender or work bowl, running the food processor for about 2 minutes. Transfer to a bowl.

Stir the soup with a wooden spoon and slowly add the light cream. When all the cream has been incorporated, taste and correct the seasonings.

Refrigerate for several hours. Serve in chilled bowls and decorate with radish slices.

Yield: 6 servings

COLD CARROT SOUP WITH YOGURT
(SLICING BLADE, BLENDER OR STEEL BLADE)

Ingredients

1 pound carrots	1½ tablespoons curry, or to
1 medium onion	taste
4 cups chicken stock or broth	1½ cups yogurt
Salt and pepper to taste	Chopped parsley for garnish
2 tablespoons butter	

Wash and scrape the carrots. Halve the onion.

Set the slicing blade in place and fit the carrots upright in the feed tube; push through to slice. Place the carrots in a saucepan, setting aside 12 slices for garnish.

Cover the carrots with the chicken stock and bring to a boil. Add salt and pepper to taste, and simmer for 15 minutes until the carrots are just tender when pierced with a fork.

Meanwhile, fit the onion in the feed tube and push through to slice.

Melt the butter in a skillet and add the onions. Sauté until the onions are cooked but not brown.

Add the curry and stir until well mixed. Remove from heat.

With a slotted spoon, transfer the carrots to the blender or work bowl, reserving 3 cups of stock. Add the onions and the yogurt and 3 cups of stock if using blender, 2 cups if using the work bowl.*

* Pour the pureed soup into a large bowl, add the final cup of chicken stock, and stir with a wooden spoon until the carrot soup is blended.

Run the food processor for 2 minutes until the vegetables are pureed and the soup is creamy and mixed well.

Refrigerate for an hour or two before serving.

To serve, pour into individual bowls and top with the reserved carrot slices and chopped parsley.

Yield: 6 servings

BLACK OLIVE SOUP
(BLENDER OR STEEL BLADE)

The scent of a single clove of garlic is quite potent in this creamy and unusual soup. Use only firm, fancy olives or, for an exceptional treat, Greek olives, drained and pitted. Since the olives can be salty, season lightly before chilling and correct the seasonings at serving time.

Ingredients

1 cup pitted ripe olives, drained
1 garlic clove
4 cups chicken stock or broth
1 tablespoon finely chopped onion

2 whole eggs
1 cup light cream
Salt and pepper to taste
2 hard-boiled eggs for garnish

Place the drained olives and the garlic clove in the blender or work bowl. Run the food processor for 1 minute until they are finely chopped. Set aside.

In a saucepan, heat the chicken stock or broth. Add the olives and garlic and simmer for 15 minutes. Add the finely chopped onions and turn the heat very low.

Place the eggs and light cream in the blender or work bowl and run the food processor for 1 minute. With the motor running, slowly pour 2 tablespoons of warm soup into the mixture to prevent it from curdling.

Slowly pour the beaten eggs and cream into the soup, stirring all the while. Season lightly with salt and pepper to taste and mix well. Chill for an hour or more in the refrigerator.

At serving time, correct the seasonings. Spoon the soup into chilled individual bowls and garnish with slices of hard-boiled egg.

Yield: 6 servings

COLD RASPBERRY SOUP
(BLENDER OR STEEL BLADE)

This sweet soup, a welcome start to a light lunch, is an inspired picnic dish. For variety, try this recipe using strawberries, blackberries, or pitted cherries.

Ingredients

2 cups raspberries, preferably
    fresh
½ cup sugar
½ cup sour cream

½ cup red wine
2 cups water
4 fresh mint leaves for garnish

Wash the raspberries well, drain, and place them in the blender or work bowl. Run the food processor for 1 minute, or until pureed.

Strain the raspberries through a fine sieve or two layers of cheesecloth, reserving the liquid.

Add the sugar, sour cream, wine, water, and the raspberry liquid to the blender or work bowl. Run the food processor for 1 minute, or until mixed well.

Remove the soup to a bowl and chill for several hours.

Serve in chilled bowls and garnish with fresh mint leaves.

Yield: 4 servings

CRANBERRY BEET SOUP
(BLENDER OR STEEL BLADE)

The essence of this sophisticated and colorful soup is the mingling of unusual ingredients: the sweetness of the beets offsets the cranberries' tartness.

Ingredients

1 pound cranberries
4 shallots
1 tablespoon butter
1 pound beets, canned with
    their liquid
3 cups chicken stock or broth

½ cup sugar
¼ cup Madeira
1 tablespoon lemon juice
Salt and pepper to taste
Lemon slices for garnish

Wash the cranberries. Set aside.

Place the shallots in the blender or work bowl. Run the food processor for 5 seconds to chop.

Melt the butter in a small skillet, and when it is hot, add the shallots. Sauté until they are transparent.

Quarter the beets and place them and their liquid in the blender or work bowl. Run the food processor until the beets are pureed.

Add the chopped shallots to the beets and run the food processor for 30 seconds. Remove the puree to a large bowl.

In a saucepan, bring the chicken stock or broth to a boil. Add the cranberries and sugar to the boiling stock and simmer for 5 minutes, or until the cranberries pop.

Put the cranberries and a cup or more of chicken stock in the blender or work bowl and run the food processor until the berries are pureed. Push the mixture through a fine sieve into the beet puree.

Add the remaining chicken stock and mix thoroughly with a wooden spoon.

Season with Madeira, lemon juice, and salt and pepper to taste.

Chill the soup for several hours. Serve garnished with lemon slices.

Yield: 6 servings

GAZPACHO
(BLENDER OR STEEL BLADE; SHREDDING BLADE)

This is our variation of gazpacho, that lively cold salad soup which can be a first course or a summer meal in itself. We like to serve gazpacho surrounded by bowls of coarsely chopped vegetables so that each person at the table can garnish and flavor the soup to his liking.

Soup Ingredients

4 ripe tomatoes
3 cucumbers
1 medium onion
1 green pepper
1 garlic clove

1 piece fresh ginger to make
   1 teaspoon chopped
2 tablespoons olive oil
1 tablespoon vinegar
1/4 teaspoon cumin
2 cups cold chicken broth

Garnish Ingredients

2 ripe tomatoes
2 cucumbers
1 large onion

6 scallions
1 cup croutons made from
   6 slices of white bread

Prepare all the vegetables for the food processor, setting aside those to be used for garnish.

—Wash the tomatoes and quarter them.
—Peel the cucumbers and cut in 4 pieces.
—Peel and quarter the onions.
—Quarter and seed the green pepper.
—Wash and trim the scallions.

Peel a piece of fresh ginger and place in the blender or work bowl. Run the food processor for 1 minute, or until the ginger is chopped fine. Place 1 teaspoon in a bowl and reserve the rest for another use. Add the olive oil to the ginger.

Place all the soup vegetables and the garlic clove in the blender or work bowl and run the food processor until pureed, about 2 minutes.

Start the food processor again and slowly pour the olive oil and ginger in a steady stream through the feed tube. Run the food processor until the vegetables have the consistency of a mayonnaise.

Add the vinegar and cumin to the chicken broth. With the food processor running, pour the broth through the feed tube. Stop the food processor when all the broth has been added and the soup is thoroughly mixed.

Pour the gazpacho into a bowl and refrigerate for at least 2 hours before serving.

Meanwhile, prepare the vegetables for garnish:

In your blender or work bowl, coarsely chop, separately, the tomatoes (2 or 3 seconds), the cucumbers (3 seconds), the onion (3 seconds), and the scallions (15 seconds). Place each variety of vegetable in a separate bowl and chill until serving time.

Prepare the croutons shortly before serving time:

Preheat the oven to 325°.
Cut the bread into ½-inch cubes and spread on a baking sheet. Sprinkle with salt and pepper and bake the croutons for a few minutes, turning once or twice.

When they are golden, transfer the croutons to a bowl.

Serve the gazpacho in large chilled bowls surrounded by the small bowls of chopped vegetables and croutons.

Yield: 6 servings

Entrees

BRISKET OF BEEF WITH CRANBERRIES AND GREEN PEPPERCORNS

(BLENDER OR STEEL BLADE; SLICING BLADE)

Ingredients

6-pound brisket of beef
2 large onions
3 carrots
1 celery stalk
6 garlic cloves
½ teaspoon thyme
½ teaspoon ground cumin
1 teaspoon salt
1 teaspoon pepper
2 tablespoons lemon juice
3 tablespoons vinegar
5 tablespoons oil
½ cup white wine or dry
  vermouth

3 slices bacon
1 onion, peeled and stuck with
  3 cloves
2 cups beef stock or broth
1 15-ounce package whole
  cranberries
¾ cup sugar
½ cup water
3 tablespoons fresh green
  peppercorns, drained*
3 tablespoons butter
½ cup heavy cream
Parsley sprigs and chopped
  parsley for garnish

Marinate the beef:

Peel the onions and cut to fit the feed tube. Scrape the carrots, and wash and trim the celery.

Set the slicing blade in place. Fit the onions, carrots, and celery in the feed tube and push through to slice. Remove the vegetables to a bowl large enough to hold the brisket.

* Fresh green peppercorns, canned or in bottles, can be found in many specialty food stores.

In the blender or work bowl, place 4 garlic cloves, the thyme, cumin, salt, pepper, lemon juice, vinegar, oil, and wine or vermouth. Run the food processor for 1 minute.

Pour the marinade into the bowl with the vegetables and mix well.

Add the beef and marinate, turning once or twice, for 3 hours on the counter top or overnight in the refrigerator.

Cook the beef:

Cut the remaining garlic cloves into slivers.

Remove the meat from the marinade and make 5 or 6 slits with a knife blade. Push the garlic slivers into the slits.

Cut the bacon into 1-inch squares. In a saucepan or casserole large enough to hold the brisket, sauté the bacon until crisp. Remove the bacon from the fat and reserve for other uses.

Brown the brisket in bacon fat on all sides.

Meanwhile, pour the marinade through a strainer into a bowl; set aside. Reserve the onions.

When the brisket is browned, add the onion stuck with cloves and the onions from the marinade to the casserole.

Pour the strained marinade over the meat and bring it to a boil. Lower the heat and simmer, covered, for 1 hour.

Add 1 or 2 cups of beef stock or broth to the pot and let the meat simmer, covered, for another hour, or until the meat is tender when pierced with a fork.

Remove the brisket to a platter, cover, and keep warm while making the sauce.

Prepare the sauce:

Strain the juices that the brisket cooked in through a sieve; return to the saucepan or casserole and set aside.

Wash the cranberries and place in a small saucepan. Add the sugar and water, and bring to a boil. Lower the flame and cook the cranberries, at a low boil, until they have popped their skins.

Using a slotted spoon, reserve 1 cup of whole cranberries.

Pour the rest of the cranberries and their juices into the blender or work bowl and run the food processor for about 15 seconds until pureed.

Pour the cranberry puree into the saucepan with the meat juices.

Add green peppercorns and butter to the sauce and heat through. Add salt to taste.

Stir in the cream and correct the seasonings.

To serve:

Carve the brisket into thin slices and arrange on a platter, decorated with parsley sprigs. Spoon 3 or 4 tablespoons of sauce over the meat and pour on the reserved whole cranberries. Sprinkle with chopped parsley. Serve the remaining sauce alongside in a sauceboat.

Yield: 8 to 10 servings

PAUPIETTES OF BEEF WITH FOYOT SAUCE
(BLENDER OR STEEL BLADE)

Here is a special dish that you need never worry over. The paupiettes, or rolled steaks, can be prepared as much as a day in advance, then wrapped and refrigerated until cooking time; the Foyot Sauce will keep nicely for several hours when set in a pan of tepid water. If the butter is well chilled so that it melts at the very last moment, it takes only 6 minutes, under a very hot broiler, to cook the paupiettes to perfection—charred on the outside, rare and juicy inside.

The Paupiettes

Ingredients

3 tablespoons butter, cut in
   small pieces

3 garlic cloves

12 basil leaves, or ½ teaspoon
   dried basil

Salt and pepper to taste

6 slices round steak, about
   ¼ inch thick

6 slices lean bacon

In the blender or work bowl, place the butter, garlic cloves, and basil and run the food processor for 40 seconds, or until the butter is creamed. Add salt and pepper to taste and run the food processor for a second to mix.

Transfer the butter to a bowl and chill in the refrigerator for 2 hours, or in the freezer for 30 minutes.

When well chilled, divide the butter into 6 pieces. Line up the steaks and place a mound of butter in the center of each.

Roll the steaks so that they look like small, fat sausages. Wrap with a slice of bacon and secure with a toothpick.

Refrigerate if preparing ahead.

The Foyot Sauce

Ingredients

1 cup Béarnaise Sauce
   (see page 174)

¼ teaspoon Bovril or other
   concentrated meat extract

In the blender or work bowl, prepare Béarnaise Sauce.

To the Béarnaise, add Bovril or other concentrated meat extract. Run the food processor for only a fraction of a second, or stir in with a wooden spoon. Taste and correct the seasonings.

Pour the Foyot Sauce into a bowl or sauceboat. If preparing ahead, keep warm in a pan of tepid water.

To serve:

Preheat the broiler.

When the broiler is very hot, place the rolled steaks about 3 inches from the flame and cook them for 3 minutes. Turn and cook for 3 minutes more.

Remove the toothpicks and place the paupiettes on a serving platter decorated with watercress. Serve the Foyot Sauce in a sauceboat.

Yield: 6 servings

FILET MIGNON STUFFED WITH MARROW
(BLENDER OR STEEL BLADE)

Though 1½-inch-thick filet mignons will more than suffice, this dish can be even more luxuriant if you buy a whole filet, trim it yourself, and prepare steaks 2 to 2½ inches thick. One tablespoon of marrow filling per filet is a subtle and unusual contribution. The mushrooms for the sauce should melt in your mouth and be chopped rather fine, as for duxelles, but not so fine as to be mushy. Spoon most of the sauce around, not over, the steaks and garnish the platter with watercress sprigs. For added color, top each steak, at the last minute, with a bit of tarragon butter.

Ingredients

6 beef marrow bones or
   6 tablespoons marrow
3 tablespoons dried tarragon
Salt and pepper to taste
6 filet mignons
6 strips bacon or fatback
6 tablespoons butter

2 tablespoons cognac or brandy
1 pound mushrooms, washed
   and trimmed
3 shallots
½ cup beef stock or bouillon
Watercress for garnish
Tarragon butter, optional (see
    page 121)

Rinse the marrow bones under cold running water. Place them in a saucepan, cover with water, and bring to a boil. Lower the flame and simmer for 15 minutes until the marrow is soft and white.

Drain the bones and, when they are cool enough to handle, remove the marrow by tapping the bones on a counter top, or scrape around the inside with a knife; the marrow should fall out easily.

In the blender or work bowl, place the marrow and 2 tablespoons of tarragon. Run the food processor for 2 seconds to puree. Transfer to a bowl and season well with salt and pepper. Taste and correct the seasonings, adding a bit more tarragon if desired.

Chill the marrow in the refrigerator for 20 minutes or so to harden.

Meanwhile, trim or have the butcher trim 6 filet mignons, cutting away any outer fat.

Cut a deep slit in the side of each filet, leaving an opening just wide enough to spoon the stuffing through.

Place 1 tablespoon of marrow stuffing in each filet.

Wrap a strip of bacon or fatback around the circumference of each steak. Secure the bacon with two pieces of kitchen string so that each filet will be nice and round and can be browned on all sides.*

In a heavy skillet, melt the butter. When the butter is very hot and begins to color, add the filets and brown on all sides.

Pour cognac over and ignite. When the flame dies down, lower the heat and cook the steaks to the desired doneness.

Remove the filets to a platter and keep warm while preparing the sauce.

In the blender or work bowl, place the mushrooms and shallots and run the food processor for about 5 seconds to chop medium fine.

In the skillet, in the butter in which the filets were cooked, sauté the mushrooms and shallots for several minutes, scraping the bottom with a wooden spoon.

* The meat can be prepared several hours ahead to this point, covered, and placed in the refrigerator till a half hour before cooking time.

To the mushrooms and shallots, add the beef stock or bouillon, the remaining tarragon, and salt and pepper to taste. Cook for 2 or 3 more minutes until the mushrooms are tender. Taste and correct the seasonings.

To serve, place the filets on a serving platter and remove the strings and, if you wish, the bacon or fatback as well. Pour most of the sauce around the meat, spooning only a bit on each steak so that the filets stay firm. If desired, place a mound of chilled tarragon butter on each steak. Decorate the platter with watercress sprigs.

Tarragon Butter

This is a finishing touch, not at all necessary but delightful with this and other red meats. The seasoned butter can be made with ease in large quantities in the blender or work bowl, frozen in a plastic container, and spooned out with a melon scoop as needed. Allow about ¼ teaspoon of dried tarragon for each tablespoon of butter, and run the food processor until the butter is creamed.

Ingredients

3 tablespoons butter
½–¾ teaspoon tarragon

Good pinch of freshly ground
  black pepper
Drop of lemon juice (optional)

Mix the ingredients together with your hands until well blended. Roll the butter between your palms to form 6 cones or "kisses."

Place the cones, upright, on a dish and chill in the freezer for 30 minutes.

At serving time, place a cone on each filet.

Yield: 6 servings

FONDUE BOURGUIGNONNE

This is a favorite for informal dining, with each guest cooking and saucing his own meat. Place the platter of raw cubed steak in the center of the table, surround it with bowls of condiments and sauces—the more, the better—and set the fondue pot nearby, where everyone can reach it. Serve with thick slices of French bread and a full-bodied red wine.

The Fondue

Ingredients

3 pounds round steak   5 tablespoons oil
2 tablespoons butter

Remove excess fat from the steak and cut into 1-inch cubes. Place in a bowl and refrigerate.

At serving time, transfer the steak to a platter, bring to the table, and surround with separate bowls filled with condiments and sauces.

Meanwhile, set out a fondue pot. When ready to serve, heat the butter and oil in the fondue pot on the stove.

When the butter is bubbling, bring the pot to the table and adjust the flame so that the butter is bubbling and hot enough to cook the beef. Let each diner spear a cube of beef with his fork, cook it quickly in the oil, and dip it in the sauce or condiment of his choice.

Yield: 6 servings

The Condiments and Sauces
(BLENDER OR STEEL BLADE; SHREDDING BLADE)

Ingredients

Freshly ground black pepper
Coarse salt
2 large onions, quartered
½ cup drained capers
1 bunch parsley
¼ pound fresh horseradish

1 cup Mayonnaise Aïoli (see below)
1 cup Dilled Mustard Sauce (see page 125)
1 cup Hot Haitian Sauce (see page 124)

Grind 2 or 3 tablespoons of black pepper into a bowl.
Pour several tablespoons of coarse salt into a bowl.

In the blender or work bowl:

Chop the onions for 10 seconds; remove to a bowl.
Chop the capers for 5 seconds; remove to a bowl.
Chop the parsley for 5 seconds; remove to a bowl.

Set the food processor with the shredding blade:

Peel the horseradish and fit in the feed tube. Push through to grate. Remove to a bowl.

Prepare the following sauces in the blender or work bowl:

Mayonnaise Aïoli

Ingredients

1 cup mayonnaise (see page 177)
1 slice white bread ¾ inch thick

3 tablespoons milk
4 garlic cloves
Juice of ½ lemon

Soak the bread in the milk in a saucer. When the milk is absorbed, wring the bread to squeeze all the milk out.

[123]

Place the garlic cloves and the bread in the blender or work bowl and run the food processor for 15 seconds until they form a paste.

Add the mayonnaise and run the food processor for 5 seconds.

With the food processor off, taste the Aïoli and correct the seasonings, adding lemon juice as desired; Aïoli should have a strong garlic and lemon flavor.

Transfer the Aïoli to a bowl and chill for at least half an hour.

Hot Haitian Sauce

Ingredients

3 tomatoes
1 celery stalk
1 medium onion, quartered
1 or 2 chili peppers
½ cup oil

4 garlic cloves
½ cup dry white wine
⅛ teaspoon ground cloves
Salt and pepper to taste

Peel and seed the tomatoes. Trim the celery and cut in several pieces.

Place the tomatoes and celery in the blender or work bowl. Add the onion and chili peppers, and run the food processor for 15 seconds.

In a saucepan, heat the oil. Add the tomato mixture and sauté over moderate heat until the vegetables are soft, about 15 minutes.

Peel the garlic and place it in the blender or work bowl. Run the food processor for 10 seconds.

Add the garlic, wine, cloves, and salt and pepper to the sauce.

Cook for 40 minutes, stirring occasionally, until the sauce is thick.

Strain the sauce through a fine sieve and keep warm until serving time.

Dill Mustard Sauce

Ingredients

10 dill sprigs
3 tablespoons wine vinegar,
  preferably white
2 tablespoons Dijon mustard

1 garlic clove
½ cup olive oil
½ cup vegetable oil

Place dill sprigs in the blender or work bowl and run the food processor for 10 seconds, or until finely chopped; set aside.

Place the vinegar, mustard, and garlic in the blender or work bowl. Run the food processor for 10 seconds.

Mix the olive and vegetable oils in a pitcher or measuring cup. Start the food processor and, very slowly at first, pour the oil through the feed tube; continue pouring in a steady stream until the sauce has the consistency of heavy cream.

Transfer the sauce into a bowl and sprinkle with minced dill. Chill until ready to serve.

GROUND STEAK AU POIVRE

(BLENDER AND MEAT GRINDER ATTACHMENT OR STEEL
BLADE; COFFEE GRINDER ATTACHMENT, OPTIONAL)

This dish is amusing, extravagant, and delicious—just right for a dinner for two. For light, juicy hamburgers, mix the meat thoroughly with your fingertips and shape quickly without kneading.

Ingredients

1 large garlic clove
1 small onion, quartered
½ teaspoon salt
1 pound sirloin, preferably, or
  round steak, cut in cubes
2 tablespoons black peppercorns

1 tablespoon butter
2 tablespoons cognac
¼ cup beef stock or broth or
  brown sauce, if available
¼ cup heavy cream

Place the garlic, onion, and salt in the blender or work bowl. Run the food processor for 30 seconds; remove to a bowl.

Trim any excess fat from the beef and cut into 1½-inch cubes. Push the steak through the medium blade of the meat grinder or place in the work bowl and run the food processor for 40 seconds, or until ground fine.

Add the ground meat to the onions and garlic and mix thoroughly.

Crack the peppercorns coarse, using a coffee grinder attachment, if desired, or place the peppercorns in a sandwich bag and hit them with a hammer, a skillet, or whatever is handy.

Shape the beef, lightly, into 2 half-inch-thick patties. Using the heel of your hand, press the peppercorns into both sides of the meat.

In a heavy skillet, melt the butter. When the butter is hot, add the beef and cook over a medium-high flame for 3 minutes for a rare hamburger, 4 minutes for medium rare. Turn and cook for 3 minutes more.

Pour the cognac over the beef and ignite. Shake the pan until the flame dies. Remove hamburgers to a warm platter.

To the skillet, add the stock or broth and boil, scraping the bottom with a wooden spoon, until the liquid is reduced by half.

Turn off the flame and stir in the heavy cream.

Pour the sauce over the hamburgers and serve immediately with homemade french fries.

Yield: 2 large servings

VEAL CHOPS PASSETTO
(BLENDER OR STEEL BLADE)

Ingredients

4 thick veal chops
1 small carrot
½ stalk celery
1 small onion
6 tablespoons butter
¾ pound mushrooms
¼ pound Westphalian ham

1½ cups tomato sauce (see
    page 188)
¼ cup white wine
2 tablespoons capers, drained
Salt and pepper to taste
Parsley for garnish

Preheat the oven to 400°.

Trim the veal chops or have the butcher do it.

Scrape the carrot and wash and trim the celery; cut in several pieces. Place the carrot, celery, and onion in the blender or work bowl and run the food processor for 15 seconds, or until finely chopped.

In a skillet, melt 3 tablespoons of butter. When it is hot, add the chopped vegetables and cook over medium heat until the onion has browned.

Meanwhile, wash and trim the mushrooms and pat dry. Place the mushrooms and the Westphalian ham in the blender or work bowl. Run the food processor for 5 seconds to chop coarsely.

Add the mushrooms and ham to the vegetables. Stir in the tomato sauce and the wine. Add the capers and season with salt and pepper to taste.

Cook the sauce over medium heat for 25 minutes, stirring frequently.

While the sauce is cooking, melt the remaining butter in a heavy skillet. When the butter is bubbling, add the veal chops and brown on both sides over a moderately high heat.

Lower to a medium heat and continue cooking the chops until almost tender.

Cut 4 squares of aluminum foil, each large enough to wrap around a chop, and place a veal chop on each square.

Cover the chop with a generous amount of sauce. Fold up the foil and seal tight.

Place the veal chops on a baking sheet and bake in a preheated 400° oven for about 10 minutes.

At serving time, place the veal chops on a serving platter and open up the foil as you would for a baked potato. Surround with parsley sprigs and serve with buttered carrots and a green salad.

Yield: 4 large servings

SCALLOP OF VEAL
WITH VEGETABLES
(BLENDER OR STEEL BLADE)

Ingredients

2 bunches carrots, scraped and
   cut in several pieces
½ cup raw rice
15 fresh basil leaves, or
   2 teaspoons dried basil
1½ teaspoons salt
1 cup water
7 tablespoons butter
12 small onions, peeled
1½ cups chicken stock or
   broth

1 bay leaf
4 parsley sprigs
Salt and pepper to taste
¾ pound mushrooms, washed
   and trimmed
6–8 tablespoons Madeira
Pinch of nutmeg
1½ pounds veal scallops
½ cup flour
2 tablespoons oil
1 teaspoon tomato paste

Cook the vegetables:

Place the carrots, in several batches, in the blender or work bowl. Run the food processor, turning it on and off, until the carrots are coarsely chopped.

[128]

Place the carrots in a saucepan. Add the rice, about 8 basil leaves (or 1 teaspoon dried basil), and 1½ teaspoons of salt. Pour in 1 cup of water and cook, covered, over low heat for 30 minutes, or until the rice is soft. Check the mixture once or twice, adding more water as necessary.

While the carrots are cooking, melt 1 tablespoon of butter in a skillet. When the butter is hot, add the onions and brown them on all sides.

Pour on 1 cup of chicken stock or broth. Add the bay leaf, the parsley sprigs, the rest of the basil, and salt and pepper to taste. Cover the skillet and cook, over a medium heat, for 25 minutes until the onions are soft. Transfer the onions and broth to a bowl.

In the same skillet, melt 2 tablespoons of butter. Add the mushrooms and sauté for a few minutes, over a fairly high heat, until the mushrooms are cooked but still crisp. Set aside.

Place the carrot-and-rice mixture in the blender or work bowl and run the food processor until the carrots are pureed. Transfer the mixture to a saucepan or the top of a double boiler.

Add 2 tablespoons of Madeira, nutmeg, and 1 tablespoon of butter to the carrots and mix well. Heat and keep warm in a pan of simmering water.

Prepare the veal:

Sprinkle the veal scallops with salt and pepper. Dust lightly with flour.

In a skillet, heat 2 tablespoons each of butter and oil. When the butter begins to bubble, add the veal and sauté until golden brown.

Remove the veal to a platter and cover with a warm plate.

Prepare the sauce:

Place 1 tablespoon of flour and 1 tablespoon of butter in the blender or work bowl and run the food processor until they form a paste. To the blender or work bowl, add the broth from the onions, ½ cup of chicken broth, 3 tablespoons of Madeira, and 1 teaspoon of tomato paste. Run the food processor for about 8 seconds, or until the sauce is well mixed.

Pour the sauce into the skillet that the veal cooked in and bring to a boil. Lower the heat and simmer for 5 minutes.

Heat the veal and vegetables:

Add the veal scallops to the sauce and simmer, over a low flame, for 10 minutes.

Season with salt and pepper to taste. Add 1 to 3 tablespoons Madeira, as desired.

Add the onions and the mushrooms to the sauce and cook only to heat through.

To serve:

Spread the carrot puree on a serving platter.

Arrange the veal scallops on top.

Make a border around the puree with the mushrooms and the onions.

Pour the sauce from the skillet over the veal and serve at once.

Yield: 6 servings

VEAL MOUSSE WITH PAPRIKA SAUCE
(MEAT GRINDER AND BLENDER, OR STEEL BLADE)

Though other sauces may be good with this pleasing veal mousse, our first choice is Paprika Sauce, all lightness and cream. When you bake the mousse slowly in a pan of water, as with pâté the water level should reach about a third of the way up the sides of the mold or loaf pan. Be sure to choose a serving platter that will hold the cooking juices, surround the mousse with parsley, and serve with the Paprika Sauce in a sauceboat on the side.

Veal Mousse

Ingredients

1 pound loin of veal	1½ cups heavy cream
1 teaspoon salt	Butter for greasing a 1½-
1 teaspoon pepper	quart mold or loaf pan
¼ teaspoon nutmeg	Parsley for garnish
2 eggs	

Preheat the oven to 375°.

If using meat grinder and blender, trim the veal and cut into 3-inch cubes. Use the fine blade, if available, or push the meat through the meat grinder twice to grind very fine. Transfer the veal to the blender.

If using steel blade, trim the veal and cut into 1½-inch cubes. Place in the work bowl and run the food processor for 40 seconds, or until chopped fine. Stop the machine.

To the ground veal add the salt, pepper, and nutmeg. Break the eggs into a bowl and get the cream ready to pour.

Start running the food processor, and, after 5 seconds, drop the eggs through the feed tube; they should be absorbed in about 3 seconds. Then, without stopping the motor, pour the heavy cream through the feed tube and continue running the food processor for 4 more seconds until well mixed.

Butter the mold or loaf pan. Pour the veal mixture into it and seal tightly with aluminum foil.

Place the mold in a shallow pan. Fill the pan with water until it reaches a third of the way up the side of the mold.

Place in a preheated 375° oven and bake for 45 minutes.

Unmold the mousse and its juices onto a platter decorated with parsley and serve, at once, with Paprika Sauce.

Yield: 6 servings

Paprika Sauce

Ingredients

1 carrot, scraped
½ stalk celery, trimmed
1 medium onion, quartered
2 shallots
5 tablespoons butter
½ teaspoon salt

1½ teaspoons paprika
1 cup white wine
2½ cups chicken stock or
  broth
1 tablespoon flour
1 cup sour cream

Clean the vegetables and cut into several pieces. Place the carrot, celery, onion, and shallots in the blender or work bowl and run the food processor for about 10 seconds, or until chopped fine.

Melt 4 tablespoons of butter in a skillet. Add the vegetables, salt, and paprika to the skillet. Cover with a lid and cook over a low heat for 20 minutes.

Add the white wine to the vegetables and cook, covered, over medium heat for 5 minutes.

Remove the lid and pour in the chicken broth. Over a high heat, reduce the mixture by half.

Strain the mixture through a very fine sieve, pressing the vegetables with the back of a wooden spoon to squeeze out their juices; discard the vegetables.

Pour the sauce into a small saucepan and bring to a boil.

Meanwhile, with your hand, blend 1 tablespoon of butter with 1 tablespoon of flour until the flour is absorbed. Add the *beurre manié* to the boiling sauce to thicken it and cook, stirring with a wooden spoon, for several minutes.

When the sauce is thick, lower the flame and simmer for 10 minutes, stirring from time to time.

At serving time, remove the saucepan from the flame and add the sour cream. Heat for 1 minute, taking care not to let the sauce boil, or the cream will curdle.

Pour into a sauceboat and serve with the veal mousse.

Yield: 3 cups

CROWN ROAST OF PORK
FILLED WITH APRICOTS
(BLENDER OR STEEL BLADE)

The Roast

Ingredients

1 crown roast of pork with
  16 chops
½ teaspoon dried thyme

1 teaspoon salt
Pepper to taste

The preliminary roasting:

Preheat the oven to 400°.

Trim any excess fat and sprinkle the roast with the thyme, salt, and pepper.

Cover the ends of the chops with twists of aluminum foil to keep them from burning. In the center, place an empty can, open at both ends, on end; this will hasten the melting of fat so that the center will brown nicely.

Place the roast in a roasting pan and cook in a 400° oven for 20 minutes.

Reduce the oven temperature to 325° and continue roasting the pork for 40 more minutes before filling the center.

The Apricot Filling

Ingredients

1 cup dried apricots
2 cups cooked rice
2 small celery stalks, trimmed
1 medium onion, quartered
3 tablespoons chopped parsley
3 tablespoons fresh chopped
  chives, or 1½ tablespoons
  dried chives

3 tablespoons melted butter
⅛ teaspoon each: thyme,
  mace, nutmeg, ground cloves
Salt and pepper to taste

Place the apricots, the cooked rice, celery, onion, parsley, and chives in the blender or work bowl. Run the food processor for 2 minutes until you have a paste.

Pour the melted butter into the apricot mixture. Add the thyme, mace, nutmeg, and ground cloves, and run the food processor for a second or two to mix. Season the filling with salt and pepper, and set aside.

Fill the roast and complete the cooking:

After it has cooked for an hour, take the roast out of the oven. Remove the can and spoon the apricot filling into the center. Cover the filling with aluminum foil to prevent it from burning.

Place the roast back in the oven and cook for 1 hour and 5 minutes, basting several times.

Remove the aluminum foil from the center and cook the roast 10 minutes more or until the outside is a dark golden brown and the juices run clear when pricked with a fork. The meat, when cut, should be white, never pink. Transfer the fully cooked crown roast to a serving platter and keep warm, at the back of the stove, while preparing the sauce.

The Sauce

Ingredients

2 tablespoons pan juices
2 tablespoons flour
½ cup dry white wine

½ cup chicken stock or broth
1 cup heavy cream

Add pan juices to a saucepan. Blend in the flour and mix well, stirring with a wooden spoon.

Cook the roux over a low heat, stirring constantly, for 2 to 3 minutes.

Add the wine, slowly, to the roux, stirring all the while. Over a high heat, reduce the wine until you have 3 tablespoons of sauce.

Spoon the sauce into the blender or work bowl. Run the food

processor and pour the chicken broth through the feed tube; continue running until well mixed.

Pour the cream through the feed tube and run the food processor for 2 seconds.

Pour the sauce into the top of a double boiler and heat through, taking care not to let the sauce boil. Taste and correct the seasonings.

To serve:

Serve the roast on a platter, decorated with watercress. If you choose, remove the foil from the chops and replace with paper frills. Serve the sauce alongside in a gravy boat.

Yield: 10 to 12 servings

PORK CHOPS, STUFFED AND SAUCED
(BLENDER OR STEEL BLADE)

Ingredients

6 double-rib pork chops
¼ pound chicken livers
¼ pound bacon
2 garlic cloves
1 cup bread crumbs made
    from stale bread
1 egg
1 tablespoon sage

1½ tablespoons rosemary
1 teaspoon oregano
Salt and pepper to taste
3 tablespoons oil
½ cup chicken stock or broth
1 cup yogurt
Parsley for garnish

Trim the pork chops, or have the butcher do it. Make a deep slit, or pocket, to be stuffed, along the side of the chop, working the knife blade back toward the bone. Pat the chops dry with paper towels and set aside.

Wash the chicken livers and remove any tendons. If using slab bacon, cut into cubes.

Place the chicken livers, bacon, and garlic cloves in the blender or work bowl and run the food processor for 1 minute until the mixture forms a thick paste.

To the liver paste, add the bread crumbs, egg, sage, rosemary, oregano, and salt and pepper to taste. Run the food processor just long enough to mix well.

Stuff each pork chop with the liver mixture. Close the slit with a skewer or toothpick and season the chop with salt and pepper.

In a heavy skillet, heat the oil. When it is hot, add the pork chops and brown them, quickly, on both sides.

Lower the heat and cook, covered, for 20 minutes until the meat is tender and white inside. Remove the chops from the skillet and keep warm, between two hot platters, at the side of the stove.

Pour off all but 2 tablespoons of pan juices. Add the chicken stock or broth to the skillet and cook, over a high heat, scraping with a wooden spoon, until the liquid is well mixed.

In the blender or work bowl, place the yogurt. Add the liquid from the skillet and run the food processor for 15 seconds.

Pour the yogurt sauce into the top of a double boiler and heat through, slowly, stirring all the while. Taste and correct the seasonings.

Serve the pork chops on a platter decorated with parsley sprigs and spoon the sauce over the chops.

Yield: 6 servings

FRESH PORK PIE
(BLENDER OR STEEL BLADE)

This simple dish is at its best steaming hot with broccoli alongside and, some days, a bit of freshly grated horseradish. Whether you plan to serve the pie hot or cold, after you have simmered the pork, be sure to sample it, adding more cloves or thyme to suit your palate. Since the olives can be saline, salt it lightly.

Ingredients

One 9-inch pie crust, top and bottom, made with pâte brisée (see page 41)
1 pound pork shoulder or fresh ham
1 medium onion, quartered
1 garlic clove
½ teaspoon thyme

¼ teaspoon each: oregano, ground cloves, salt, and pepper
¼ cup dry oatmeal
½ cup ice water
2 tablespoons oil
12–16 stuffed green olives
1 egg

Preheat the oven to 400°.

Prepare the pâte brisée. Dust the dough ball and set aside half for the top crust.

Butter a 9-inch pie plate and roll the dough to fit the plate. Refrigerate the shell while preparing the filling.

Cube the pork and push it through the meat grinder *or* place it in the work bowl and run the food processor for 1 minute.

If using the steel blade, add the onion, garlic, thyme, oregano, cloves, salt and pepper, and run the food processor for one more minute. Add the oatmeal and ice water to the mixture and run the food processor for a second or two to mix.

If using the meat grinder, transfer the meat to a bowl. Place the onion and garlic in the blender and chop for 4 seconds; add them to the meat. Add the spices to the mixture and mix thoroughly with a wooden spoon or your hands. Pour in the ice water and the oatmeal and mix well.

In a heavy skillet, heat the oil and, when it is hot, add the seasoned pork. Lower the flame and simmer the meat for 1 hour, stirring frequently.

Remove from the stove and let the mixture cool for 15 minutes. Meanwhile, drain the olives.

Remove the pastry shell from the refrigerator and fill it with a layer of ground pork.

Arrange 8 or 10 olives in a ring around the perimeter of the pie, a half inch from the crust.

Fill the pie with a second layer of ground pork.

Make a smaller circle of olives, closer to the center of the pie.

Fill the pie with the remaining ground pork.

Roll the reserved dough very thin. Cover the pie with it. Seal the edges with water, and trim off any excess dough. If you wish to decorate the top crust, make a design using the excess dough.

Beat the egg lightly with 1 tablespoon of water and, using a pastry brush, paint the crust to glaze it.

Place the pie, on a baking sheet, in a preheated 400° oven and bake for 35 minutes until the pastry is golden brown.

Serve the pie at once.

Yield: 6 servings

COLD CHICKEN FARCI EDITH FERBER
(BLENDER OR STEEL BLADE; SLICING BLADE; WHISK ATTACHMENT OR HAND BEATER)

A friend of ours developed this truly beautiful dish. Here, the chicken, once deboned, is left intact, and the stuffing spooned in to fill the space left by the carcass; then the bird is reassembled and cooked until the skin is golden brown. When chilled, the eggplant stuffing assumes a marvelous texture, so that, when sliced, the Chicken Farci appears to be an exotic pâté. To be sure that the slices are compact, serve the dish very cold, preferably after being refrigerated overnight. The pan juices, when chilled, form a jelly that serves as a sauce as well as a garnish.

Ingredients

1 small eggplant, about
  ½ pound
1 5-pound roasting chicken,
  deboned with the legs
  left on
The chicken carcass and giblets
3 tablespoons olive oil
Salt and pepper to taste
2 tablespoons cognac
2½ cups chicken stock or
  broth
½ pound mushrooms

3 chicken livers
1 medium onion, quartered
2 garlic cloves
1 egg
½ cup heavy cream
10 fresh basil leaves, or 1½
  teaspoons dried basil
1 teaspoon tarragon
¾ cup bread crumbs made
  from fresh bread
Parsley for garnish

Preheat the oven to 450°.
Bake the eggplant at 450° for 20 minutes, or until soft. Let cool to room temperature.

Prepare the chicken:

Debone the chicken, leaving the legs on and the meat as undisturbed as possible, or have the butcher debone it for you.

If doing it yourself, make a deep slit on the bottom along the backbone from the neck to the tail; all the work will be done from underneath and the slit will be sewn up later. Cut off the wings with a knife.

With a sharp knife, blade inward so as not to tear the skin, cut the meat away from the carcass, working first on one side of the chicken and then on the other. Remove the thigh bones, using poultry shears, but leave the legs on so that you will be able to reconstruct the chicken to its original shape (see illustration at top of page 140).

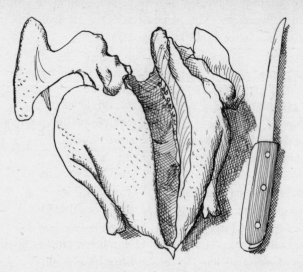

Using the knife blade to loosen any connecting tissues, remove the carcass without breaking the skin, and set aside (see illustration below).

With a needle and ordinary white thread, sew the skin closed where the wings were cut off.

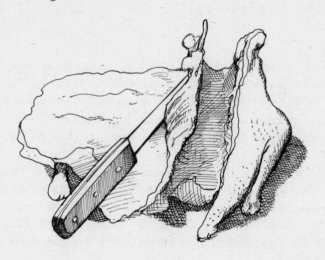

The chicken will now be one flat piece. Sprinkle it inside and out with salt and pepper and rub with the cut half of a lemon. Set the chicken aside for an hour or so until you are ready to stuff it.

Cut the chicken carcass into 5 or 6 pieces and pat dry with paper towels. Rinse off the chicken giblets and pat dry.

In a kettle or casserole large enough to hold the whole chicken, heat 2 tablespoons of olive oil. When the oil is hot, add the carcass and the giblets and brown on all sides.

Sprinkle the carcass with salt and pepper. Pour the cognac over and ignite.

When the cognac burns off, add 1 cup of stock or broth to the kettle and lower the flame to a medium heat. Cook, covered, for 20 minutes, stirring from time to time.

Prepare the stuffing while the carcass is cooking:

Wash and trim the mushrooms; drain.

Rinse the chicken livers and remove any tendons.

Slit the baked eggplant lengthwise, remove the pulp, and discard the skin. Place the pulp in the blender or work bowl and run the food processor for 2 seconds.

Pour the eggplant into a fine sieve or a layer of cheesecloth and squeeze it or push down on it with the back of a spoon to get all the water out.

Return the eggplant to the blender or work bowl. Add the mushrooms, chicken livers, onion, garlic, egg, heavy cream, basil, and tarragon. Run the food processor for 5 seconds.

Add the bread crumbs and the remaining cognac and run the food processor for a second or two to mix well. Remove the stuffing to a bowl and season with salt and pepper to taste.

Stuff the chicken:

Sew the chicken back together, starting at the tail and sewing along the back of the neck (see illustration at top of page 142). Leave an opening at the neck large enough to spoon the stuffing through.

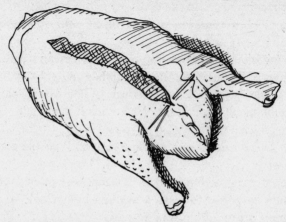

Spoon the stuffing into the chicken so that it more or less fills the space where the carcass has been removed.

Sew the neck together.

Truss the chicken and tie it with string as you would a standing roast (see illustration below).

Brown the chicken:

With a slotted spoon, remove the chicken carcass and giblets to a bowl.

To the kettle, add 1 tablespoon of oil and heat it slowly. Place the chicken gently in the kettle and brown it, over a low heat, on all sides. Take care that the heat is low or the skin will burst; if

that happens, cover the opening at once with aluminum foil so that the stuffing stays inside the bird.

When the chicken is lightly browned, add the giblets and the carcass. Pour in the remaining 1½ cups of chicken stock or broth and cook the chicken, covered, over a low heat for 35 minutes, or until tender. The chicken is done when the leg juices run clear when pricked with a fork.

Remove the kettle from the stove and let the chicken cool in its juices for several hours.

When cool, remove the chicken from the kettle and wrap tightly, to hold its shape, in aluminum foil. Refrigerate overnight.

Pour the pan juices through a strainer into a shallow pan and chill in the refrigerator until serving time.

Serve the chicken:

Remove the strings and place the chilled bird on a platter covered with parlsey. Carve 2 or 3 slices, slicing up and down, from the breast and lay them, overlapping slightly, on the platter, leading up to the whole chicken (see below).

Remove the jellied pan juices from the refrigerator. Scrape off the fat and, with a knife, cut the jelly into cubes. Arrange the cubes on the platter and, decoratively, on the slices.

Slice the remaining chicken at the table, accompanying each slice with several cubes of jellied sauce.

Yield: 6 to 8 servings

STUFFED GAME HENS
ON A BED OF CABBAGE
(MEAT GRINDER OR STEEL BLADE; SLICING BLADE)

One of our favorite ways of preparing game birds is to wrap them in bacon, brown them, then cook them for a short while on a bed of shredded cabbage. Because squab and other game birds are quite expensive, we have adapted this method to the newly available fresh cornish game hens with superb results.

Ingredients

4 rock cornish game hens,
  fresh if possible
The livers plus 7 chicken livers,
  or 8 chicken livers
2 tablespoons butter
2 tablespoons cognac
½ pound veal
1½ teaspoons sage
1 egg

½ cup bread crumbs made
  from fresh bread
1 tablespoon goose fat, if
  available (optional)
Salt and pepper to taste
10 slices bacon
1 medium head cabbage
1 cup dry white wine
Watercress for garnish

Prepare the stuffing:

Rinse off the livers, remove any tendons, and pat dry.

In a skillet, heat the butter. When the butter is hot, add the livers and sauté for a few minutes until they are light brown on the outside and still pink inside.

Pour the cognac over and ignite. When the cognac burns off, remove the skillet from the heat.

Trim the veal, if necessary, and cut into 1½-inch cubes.

—*If using the meat grinder,* push the veal and livers through once to grind coarse. Remove to a bowl. Add the sage and egg.

—*If using the steel blade,* place the veal, livers, sage, and egg in the work bowl. Run the food processor for 1 minute, or until the mixture is coarsely ground. Transfer to a bowl.

[144]

To the ground meat add the bread crumbs, goose fat (if used), and salt and pepper to taste. Mix well.

In the skillet, cook 4 slices of bacon until crisp. Remove the bacon to a paper towel and reserve the fat.

When the bacon has cooled, crumble it into the stuffing and mix.

Stuff the hens; cook the hens and the cabbage:

Wipe the cornish hens with a damp cloth; dry well.

Divide the stuffing among the 4 birds, fill, and sew the opening closed with a needle and thread, or pin closed with small skewers.

Wrap the center of each bird with a slice of bacon and tie with a piece of string.

In a large saucepan, slowly melt the remaining bacon slices. When the bacon is crisp, remove it with a slotted spoon and set aside. Add the reserved bacon fat to the saucepan.

Place the hens in the saucepan and brown well on all sides over medium heat. After about 15 minutes, or when the surrounding bacon strips are crisp, remove the birds to a platter.

Meanwhile, set the slicing blade in place.

Cut the cabbage head into quarters, remove the core, and cut each section in two. Separate the sections once more, this time into outer leaves and inner leaves.

For nice long shreds, do not stuff the cabbage into the feed tube. Instead, start the food processor and drop the cabbage into the feed tube and push through. Continue until all the cabbage is shredded.

After removing the hens from the saucepan, add the cabbage, the reserved bacon, and salt and pepper. Cook over medium heat for 10 minutes, stirring all the while.

Pour in the white wine and mix well.

Place the hens on the cabbage and sprinkle them with salt and pepper.

Cover the saucepan, lower the heat, and cook the hens gently for 10 to 15 minutes, or until their juices run clear when pricked with a fork.

To serve, spread the cabbage on a serving platter and place the hens on top. Remove the surrounding bacon and string. Decorate the platter with watercress and serve at once.

Yield: 4 servings

CHICKEN CURRY TABINTA
(BLENDER OR STEEL BLADE; SLICING BLADE)

This Indonesian chicken curry is hot enough for our palates, though not for all. Should you choose to make it hotter, add more of the spices and perhaps another chili pepper. Serve with rice, a mild salad such as cucumber and yogurt, and plenty to drink.

Ingredients

1 3-pound chicken
1 2-inch piece of ginger, peeled
6 garlic cloves
5 dried red chili peppers
½ teaspoon each: ground coriander, cumin, allspice

¼ teaspoon turmeric
1 cup yogurt
2 medium onions
6 tablespoons butter
4 strands saffron
Juice of 1 lime

Wash and dry the chicken and cut into small serving pieces. Place in a bowl.

In the blender or work bowl, place the ginger, garlic, chili peppers, coriander, cumin, allspice, and turmeric. Run the food processor for 10 seconds.

Add the yogurt to the blender or work bowl and run the food processor for 10 seconds more.

Pour the yogurt sauce over the chicken and marinate for 1 hour, turning occasionally.

Set the slicing blade in place. Fit the onions into the feed tube and push through to slice.

In a heavy skillet, melt the butter. Add the onions and sauté until they are soft and brown, but not burned.

Set the blender or steel blade in place. Add the onions and butter and run the food processor until the onions form a paste.

Place the chicken and the yogurt marinade in a large saucepan that has a tight-fitting lid. Spoon the onion paste over.

Soak the saffron strands in a small saucer filled with water for a minute or so until soft. Add the saffron to the saucepan.

Pour or squeeze the lime juice over the chicken.

Cover the saucepan and cook the chicken over a medium heat for 35 minutes, or until tender.*

Serve straight from the pot.

Yield: 6 servings

* This dish can be cooked in advance and reheated with ease. It will keep for 2 or 3 days in the refrigerator.

ROAST DUCK ON A BED OF SPINACH
(BLENDER OR STEEL BLADE; SLICING BLADE)

This crispy, fat-free duck, salted and seasoned for 24 hours, is no trouble to cook; it need be turned only twice as it roasts. Since ducks more than 4½ pounds are rather fatty, we recommend preparing 2 ducks for 5 or more persons. The spinach must be cooked at the last minute. Once the duck is done, cut the bird into serving pieces and set it in the oven with the heat turned off. Then start the spinach; it should take only 2 to 3 minutes.

The Duck

Ingredients

2 ducks, 3–4½ pounds each
6 garlic cloves

1 teaspoon freshly ground
   pepper
4 tablespoons coarse salt

The day before, wipe the duck inside and out with paper towels. Remove any loose fat, especially from the cavity; the duck fat may be frozen for future use.

Place the garlic cloves, pepper, and salt in the blender or work bowl and run the food processor for about 30 seconds, or until the garlic is finely chopped.

Rub the duck, inside and out, with the mixture.

Place the duck on a platter and chill, uncovered, in the refrigerator for 24 hours; this will dry out the skin, rendering it very crisp when cooked.

The following day, preheat the oven to 400°.

Brush off excess salt from the duck.

Prick the skin all over with a fork, about every inch or two, so the fat will run free.

Place the duck on a rack in a roasting pan and moisten the bottom of the pan with ½ cup of water.

Place the duck in a preheated 400° oven for about 1½ hours.

Turn the duck twice as it cooks.

When the skin is golden brown and the juices run clear, remove the duck from the oven and cut it into serving pieces.

Turn off the oven heat and return the duck to the oven while cooking the spinach.

The Spinach

Ingredients

4 pounds fresh spinach
½ cup bread crumbs from
   good white bread

2 tablespoons olive oil
2 garlic cloves
Salt and pepper to taste

Wash the spinach, removing any stems, and dry well.

Set the slicing blade in place to shred the spinach. For nice, long shreds, place 2 or 3 leaves in the feed tube, and push through. Continue until all the spinach is shredded.

If you are not cooking the spinach immediately, set it in a bowl so that excess moisture will be released. Before cooking, squeeze the spinach gently between paper towels to remove any water.

When you are ready to remove the duck from the oven, heat the oil in a saucepan.

Slice the garlic and sauté it in the hot oil for a minute or so until it begins to brown.

Once the duck has been cut into serving pieces, add the spinach, bread crumbs, and salt and pepper to taste to the saucepan and sauté, stirring frequently, for 2 to 3 minutes, or until the spinach is heated through and still crisp rather than wilted.

To serve, spread the spinach on a platter, arrange the duck cut in serving pieces on top, and bring to the table at once.

Yield: 6 to 8 servings

STUFFED LEG OF LAMB
IN HERB PASTRY

This leg of lamb, in its crisp golden crust, is a marvelous tour de force: the shank bone is removed and replaced by hard-boiled eggs surrounded by carrots, then the meat is shaped so that it appears to be a roast with the bone in. If you carve the meat up and down as you would a standing roast, the illusion of having the bone in will be complete. When you have the butcher butterfly the lamb for you, ask him to leave the ankle bone attached, if possible, for an even more beautiful dish.

Herb Pastry
(PASTRY OR WHISK ATTACHMENT OR STEEL OR PLASTIC BLADE)

Ingredients

2 cups flour
4 tablespoons butter cut in
   small pieces
1 egg yolk

1 teaspoon salt
2 teaspoons tarragon
2 tablespoons lemon juice
½ cup ice water

In the mixing bowl, set with the pastry or whisk attachments, or in the work bowl, place the flour, butter, egg yolk, salt, and tarragon. Run the food processor for several minutes until the ingredients are well blended.

Add the lemon juice to the ice water and, with the food processor running, pour the liquid in a stream into the dough. Continue running the food processor until the dough forms a coarse meal.

Stop the machine. Remove the dough and shape it into a ball with your hands. Dust the dough with flour, wrap in waxed paper, and refrigerate for at least an hour.

Leg of Lamb
(SLICING BLADE; BLENDER OR STEEL BLADE)

Ingredients

4-pound leg of lamb,
   butterflied
4 large carrots
3 tablespoons butter
⅔ cup chopped parsley

1 tablespoon tarragon
Salt and pepper
4 hard-boiled eggs
1 egg yolk beaten with 1
   tablespoon water

Preheat the oven to 400°.

Set the slicing blade in place. Scrape the carrots and cut to fit the feed tube. Stand upright in feed tube and push through to slice.

In a skillet, melt 2 tablespoons of butter. When the butter is hot, add the carrots, parsley, tarragon, and salt and pepper to taste. Cook for 5 minutes, or until the carrots are barely tender. Remove from the heat and let cool until the carrots can be handled.

Unfold the roast and sprinkle the inside with salt and pepper.

Along the center, more or less where the bone has been removed, line up the hard-boiled eggs.

Place the carrots along the eggs (see illustration below) as you roll the roast.

Roll the lamb, tightly at the small end and more loosely at the larger end, shaping it so that it resembles a leg of lamb with the bone in. Tie at intervals with string.

Sprinkle with salt and pepper and set in a shallow roasting pan. Roast for 30 minutes in a preheated 400° oven.

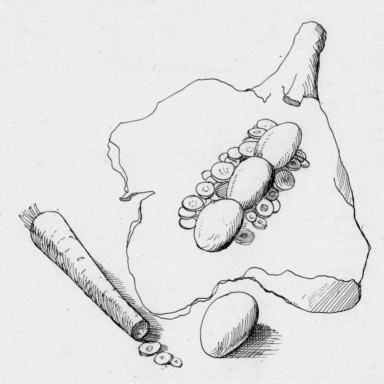

Remove the lamb from the oven and let cool to room temperature before wrapping in dough. When cool, remove the strings.*

To wrap and roast the lamb:

Preheat the oven to 400°.

Retrieve the herb pastry from the refrigerator and, with a floured rolling pin, roll the dough into a rectangle large enough to cover the entire roast.

Place the lamb, topside down, on the dough (see illustration above). Fold the dough around it so that the seams are on the bottom; the seams should overlap slightly.

---

* The lamb can be prepared ahead, even the night before, to this point. If preparing ahead, be certain to remove the lamb from the refrigerator 2 hours before cooking time so that it reaches room temperature.

Cut off any excess dough and, when you have turned the roast right-side up, make a design on top with the excess dough (see illustration below).

Wrap the roast in aluminum foil and place in the refrigerator for 15 minutes.

When the dough is firm, retrieve the roast and remove the foil. Paint the dough with the egg yolk beaten with water.

Roast the lamb in a shallow pan in a 400° oven for 1 hour for a medium-rare roast.

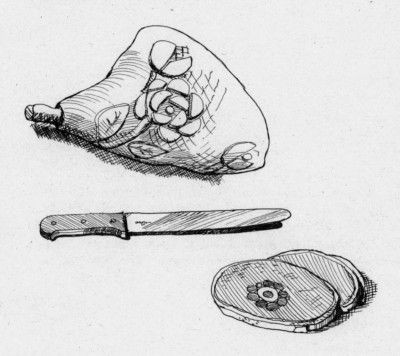

When the pastry is golden, place the roast on a platter and surround with watercress. Present whole as soon as possible, before the juices begin to seep out.

Carve the lamb away from the table in thin slices, slicing up and down, as you would a roast beef. Reassemble the slices on the platter and surround with the crust.

Accompany with parslied string beans or spinach and a good red wine.

Yield: 6 to 10 servings

LAMB RAGOUT
(SLICING BLADE)

This basic ragout, just right for a cold winter's night, is especially good when the lamb is seared and nicely browned. For variety, other vegetables—including turnips, green beans, peas, or potatoes —can be added, or a cup of wine substituted for a cup of broth. As the stew simmers, taste it and, if it seems on the sweet side, add a pinch more thyme or a crushed garlic clove. Serve this traditional dish with boiled potatoes, a green salad, and a red wine.

Ingredients

6 ounces dried brown
  mushrooms (see Note on
  page 155)
2½ pounds lamb's neck or
  other lamb stew meat
3 medium carrots
2 medium onions
3 tablespoons oil

2 tablespoons cognac
2 tablespoons flour
3 cups beef stock or broth
1 teaspoon thyme
2 bay leaves
Salt and pepper to taste
1 tablespoon soy sauce
3 tablespoons chopped parsley

Soak the dried mushrooms in warm water for 1 hour.

Meanwhile, wash the lamb under running water and pat dry with paper towels. If using stew meat other than the neck, cut into 2-inch cubes or have the butcher do it.

Scrape the carrots and cut to fit feed tube. Set the slicing blade in place, stand the carrots upright in the feed tube, and push through to slice; set aside.

Fit the onions in the feed tube and push through to slice.

In a large kettle or casserole, heat the oil. When it is hot, add the onions and cook, stirring with a wooden spoon, until they are transparent.

Add the lamb to the kettle and brown on all sides.

Pour the cognac over the seared lamb and ignite.

Sprinkle flour over the meat, stirring until the meat is coated. Continue to stir with a wooden spoon until the flour begins to brown.

Pour on the stock or broth. Add the thyme, bay leaves, and salt and pepper to taste, and bring the stock to a boil. Lower the flame and simmer, covered, for 1 hour, stirring from time to time.

Add the carrots and dried mushrooms and simmer for 25 minutes longer, or until the carrots are tender.

Skim off the fat before serving and correct the seasonings.*

Before serving, reheat, if necessary, and add soy sauce for color. At the last minute, sprinkle with chopped parsley.

Yield: 6 servings

Note: Dried brown mushrooms, usually Polish, are available at many supermarkets as well as specialty food shops.

* Lamb ragout can be prepared ahead to this point and frozen or stored in the refrigerator for 5 or 6 days.

TARTE AUX MOULES
(BLENDER OR STEEL BLADE)

Plump, juicy mussels make this tart the high point of an otherwise simple meal. The pie crust can be prepared far in advance; the mussels and sauce early in the day; and the tart assembled and baked, with ease, at the last minute. Since this is quite a filling dish, you need serve it with only a green salad and a cold white wine.

Ingredients

One 8- or 9-inch tart shell
    made with pâte brisée
    (see page 41)
3 pounds mussels
¾ cup grated Gruyère cheese
½ cup bread crumbs made
    from fresh bread
3 tablespoons chopped parsley
1 medium onion, quartered
5 tablespoons butter

1 sprig thyme, or ½ teaspoon
    dried thyme
1 teaspoon freshly ground
    black pepper
¾ cup white wine
2 tablespoons flour
½ cup heavy cream
Salt and pepper to taste
Juice of ½ lemon

Prepare the mussels and the sauce:

Wash the mussels well under cold running water. Remove the beards with a knife and scrape the shells, when necessary, with a wire brush. Set aside.

Using the blender or work bowl, grate the cheese, prepare the bread crumbs, chop the parsley, and chop the onions, separately, and remove each to a bowl.

In a large kettle melt 2 tablespoons of butter. When the butter is hot, add the onions and sauté until they are transparent and soft.

To the kettle add the parsley, thyme, and freshly ground pepper. Cover with ½ cup of white wine and bring to a boil.

When the wine is boiling, add the mussels. Steam the mussels, covered, shaking up the kettle several times, for about 8 minutes until the shells open. Discard any mussels that do not open.

Transfer the mussels to a bowl to cool and reserve the broth. When the shells are cool enough to handle, remove the mussels from the shells and set aside.

Strain the mussel broth into a saucepan through two layers of cheesecloth. Cook the broth over a medium flame until it is reduced to 1½ cups.

Place 2 tablespoons of butter and 2 tablespoons of flour in the blender or work bowl. Run the food processor for 15 seconds until well blended.

With the food processor running, slowly pour in the broth.

Then, without stopping the motor, pour the remaining wine through the feed tube.

Pour the mixture into a saucepan and bring to a boil. Reduce the heat and simmer, stirring constantly with a wooden spoon, until the mixture is the consistency of a thick cream.

Stir in the heavy cream and cook the sauce for 1 minute, taking care not to let it boil.

Remove from heat, and add the mussels to the sauce. Season with salt and pepper to taste and lemon juice. Correct the seasonings.

Assemble and bake the tart:

Preheat the oven to 400°.

Sprinkle half the grated cheese over the bottom of the tart shell.

Spoon the mussels and the sauce over this.

Mix the remaining grated cheese with the bread crumbs and sprinkle the mixture over the top of the tart.

Melt the remaining butter and drip it over the filling.

[157]

Place the pie in a preheated 400° oven and bake for 15 minutes, or until the bread crumbs are golden.

Serve at once.

Yield: 6 to 8 servings

TROUT WITH CUCUMBER STUFFING
(BLENDER OR STEEL BLADE)

Ingredients

6 brook or river trout or a 4- to 6-pound trout (see Note on page 159)
7 tablespoons butter
Salt and pepper to taste
1 medium onion, quartered
2 cucumbers

3 ounces blanched almonds, or ½ cup chopped almonds
4 cups bread crumbs made from fresh bread
2 cups white wine
Parsley and lemon for garnish

Preheat the oven to 350°.

Clean and debone the trout, leaving the heads on, or have the fishmonger do it.

Rub the cavities to be stuffed with 3 tablespoons of butter and sprinkle with salt and pepper; set aside.

Place the onion in the blender or work bowl and chop for 4 seconds.

In a skillet, heat 4 tablespoons of butter and, when it is hot, add the onions. Sauté until they are cooked but not brown.

Meanwhile, peel the cucumbers and cut into 5 pieces. Place in the blender or work bowl and run the food processor for 8 seconds to chop fine; remove to a large bowl.

Wipe out the blender or work bowl and pour the almonds into it. Run the food processor for 15 seconds, or until finely chopped. Add to the cucumbers.

Add the bread crumbs to the cucumbers and mix well.

Add the sautéed onion and butter to the bowl and mix.

Pour ½ cup of wine into the stuffing and season with salt and pepper to taste. Correct the seasonings and mix again.

Spoon the stuffing into the cavities. Close the cavities with toothpicks.

Place the fish in a baking pan and cover with 1 cup of white wine.

Bake in a preheated 350° oven, basting several times with the remaining white wine, for about 35 minutes, or until the flesh is firm and the skin loose.

Serve on a platter decorated with parsley sprigs and lemon wedges.

Yield: 6 servings

Note: If you choose to make this dish with a larger fish, follow the directions above, but rub the cavity with ½ tablespoon of butter per pound of fish and cook for 40 minutes, or until firm. This is also a good stuffing for a large flounder or bluefish.

BLUEFISH EN CROÛTE
(BLENDER OR STEEL BLADE)

This festive dish looks spectacular—and is much less difficult to prepare than you would suspect. We fill the bluefish with shrimp and fresh herbs, wrap it in pastry, and shape the dough to follow the form of the fish. Once the pastry has been decorated and glazed, the results are dazzling.

To serve 6 or 8 persons, we suggest serving 2 fish, 1½ to 2 pounds, rather than one large fish, since a big fish can be cumbersome. Should you wish to prepare this dish for 4 persons, choose a 2- to 2½-pound fish to be on the safe side.

Ingredients

Double quantity of pâte
    brisée (see page 41)
2 1½- to 2-pound bluefish
1 pound small shrimp
1 lemon
3 tablespoons butter
1 bunch parsley, washed,
    trimmed, and dried

15 fresh basil leaves, or 2
    teaspoons dried basil
3 eggs
½ cup bread crumbs made
    from fresh bread
Salt and pepper to taste
1 bunch watercress for garnish
Oil for greasing foil

Prepare two batches of pâte brisée. Dust each ball lightly with
flour and set aside. Do not refrigerate.

Have the fishmonger clean and debone 2 bluefish, leaving the
head and tail intact.

Wipe the fish with a damp cloth and pat dry. Rub each cavity
with the cut end of a lemon, squeezing out the juice. Sprinkle inside with salt and pepper and set the fish aside.

Plunge the shrimp in their shells into 1½ quarts salted boiling
water and cover. When the water returns to a boil, cook over
medium heat for 8 minutes; do not overcook.

Drain the shrimp in a colander. When cool enough to handle,
shell and devein.

Melt the butter.

In the blender or work bowl, place the shrimp, parsley—stems
and all—basil, and 2 eggs. Run the food processor for 30 seconds.

Add the melted butter and the bread crumbs and run the food
processor for 5 seconds.

Transfer the finely chopped shrimp to a bowl and season with
salt and pepper; the filling should be quite peppery.

Spoon the stuffing into the cavity of each fish and pull the cavities closed with your hands.

Preheat the oven to 375°.

Now, on a floured board, roll half the pâte brisée into a rectangle large enough to wrap around the first fish.

Place the fish along one side of the dough with the belly lined up along the edge. Fold the dough over the fish and push down along the dorsal fin until the dough conforms to the outline of the fish. As you push down, the outline of the head and tail will be revealed and you will end up with excess dough beneath the fish belly (see illustration below).

Cut off any extra dough and, following the contour of the fish belly and underside, seal the seam, moistening the edge with a little water. Press down with your thumbs to seal tightly.

Once you have successfully wrapped the fish in the pâte brisée, press down on the dough with your palms. Continue to press, with your palms, over the whole side of the fish until the outline of the fish—the head, eyes, gills—shows through.

With the back of a knife blade, draw lines on the fish tail. If necessary, use the back of the knife to press on the dough so that the configuration of the head and gills is well defined.

Draw scales on the body with a demitasse spoon (see illustration).

When the decorations please you, brush the pastry with an egg beaten with 1 tablespoon of water.

Roll the dough for the second fish and proceed, as above.

Cover a baking sheet with two large pieces of heavy-duty aluminum foil, one for each fish, and grease lightly with oil.

Place the fish on the greased foil and bake, at 375°, for about 35 minutes, or until the pastry is golden brown.

When the fish are cooked, decorate a serving platter with watercress. Then, taking care not to break the fragile dough, ease each fish onto the platter by slowly sliding it down the aluminum foil and guiding with a spatula.

Bring the platter to the table and serve at once. Slice across the fish, giving one person a piece with the tail; the head is generally for decoration. Each fish should provide 3 to 4 slices.

Serve with creamed sorrel and a chilled dry white wine.

Yield: 6 to 8 servings

LOBSTER SOUFFLÉ IN CREPES
WITH COULIS SAUCE

This truly grand dish, well worth the challenge, uses the whole lobster: the Coulis Sauce is made, at the last minute, from the pulverized shell. The soufflé, sublime by itself, is spooned onto crepes that are then folded to form half-moons. As the lobster soufflé rises, the crepes puff up and turn golden. Be prepared to serve the crepes at once on a platter decorated with parsley sprigs. Accompany with the Coulis Sauce in a sauceboat.

The Crepes
(BLENDER OR STEEL BLADE)

Ingredients

¾ cup flour
¾ cup milk
3 eggs
Pinch of salt

2 tablespoons melted butter
1 pat of butter for greasing
    the crepe pan

Place the ingredients in the blender or work bowl and run the processor for 2 minutes. If flour sticks to the sides of the container, stop the machine and scrape it down with a rubber spatula. Run the food processor for 1 minute more.

Pour the batter into a bowl and let stand for at least 1 hour.*

To cook the crepes, melt the pat of butter in a crepe pan. When the butter bubbles, pour in 3 tablespoons of batter and quickly tilt and rotate the pan until the batter covers the entire surface.

When the edges begin to brown, turn the crepe with a spatula and heat the other side for a few seconds.

Slide the crepe onto a dish.

Repeat, without rebuttering the pan, until you have used up all the batter.

Stack, cover with a bowl, and place the crepes on the side of the stove until you are ready to stuff them.

Yield: 14 to 16 crepes

* Though the crepe batter must stand for at least an hour, it can be prepared as early as the night before, then covered and refrigerated. Since the crepes will be reheated, you can prepare them in the morning and stack them until needed: be sure to keep the crepes from sticking together by separating with sheets of waxed paper or by covering the stack with a damp cloth. If you prefer keeping the crepes warm, stack them on a dish, cover with a bowl, and place in a slow oven (about 225°) for an hour, or on the side of the stove for several hours.

The Soufflé

(BLENDER OR STEEL BLADE; WHISK ATTACHMENT OR HAND BEATER; FOLDING ATTACHMENT, IF AVAILABLE)

Ingredients

1 live 2-pound lobster
Salt and pepper to taste
¼ teaspoon paprika
1 carrot
1 celery stalk
3 sprigs parsley
3 shallots

6 tablespoons butter
2 tablespoons cognac
1 cup dry white wine
2 tablespoons flour
¾ cup heavy cream
2 egg yolks
3 egg whites

Plunge the lobster in boiling water to kill it.

Cut the lobster in half with a knife and remove the intestinal vein, the small sac or craw in the head, and the spongy respiratory tissue.

Sprinkle the meat, still in its shell, with salt, pepper, and paprika, and set the lobster aside.

Scrape the carrot; wash and trim the celery, and cut in several pieces. Place the carrot, celery, parsley sprigs, and shallots in the blender or work bowl. Run the food processor for 1 minute.

In a 12-inch skillet, melt 4 tablespoons of butter. Add the chopped vegetables and sauté until they are cooked but not brown.

Meanwhile, in a small saucepan, heat the cognac.

Place the lobster on the vegetables, pour on the cognac, and ignite.

When the flame burns off, pour in the wine.

Steam the lobster, covered, over a medium flame, for 10 minutes. Remove the lobster to a bowl to cool off.

In the meantime, strain the broth the lobster cooked in, discarding the vegetables, and return the broth to the skillet. Cook over a high heat until reduced to ¼ cup.

Place 2 tablespoons of butter and the flour in the blender or work bowl and run the food processor until they form a smooth paste.

With the food processor running, pour the broth slowly through the feed tube.

Add the cream in a steady stream and continue running the food processor until the sauce is well blended.

Pour the sauce into a saucepan and bring to a boil, stirring all the while with a wooden spoon. Lower the flame to a small light.

Beat the egg yolks lightly.

Add the yolks, little by little, to the sauce, stirring constantly. When the yolks are completely absorbed, remove the sauce from the heat. Pour into a large bowl and let cool.

Remove the lobster meat from the shells and place in the blender or work bowl. Run the food processor for 1 minute, or until chopped fine. Set aside the shells and any roe for the Coulis Sauce.

Add the lobster meat to the cool cream sauce.*

Beat the egg whites with a pinch of salt until stiff using the whisk attachment or a hand beater.

To complete the lobster soufflé, when the sauce is cool, gently fold the whites in, using a wooden spoon, or, if your food processor has one, the folding attachment.

Assemble and bake the crepes:

Preheat the oven to 400°.

Place a mound of soufflé in the center of each crepe.

Fold the crepes in half.

Place the crepes, in a single layer, on a buttered baking dish. Place in a preheated 400° oven and bake for 15 minutes, or until the soufflé rises; some of the crepes may open slightly. While the crepes are baking, prepare the Coulis Sauce.

When the crepes are a light gold, arrange them on a serving platter and surround with parsley sprigs. Serve immediately with the Coulis Sauce.

Yield: 6 to 8 servings

---

* The soufflé may be prepared an hour or two ahead of time to this point.

The Coulis Sauce
(BLENDER OR STEEL BLADE)

Ingredients

The lobster shells
2 tablespoons butter
¼ cup cognac

1 cup fish stock or chicken
  broth or bouillon
1 tablespoon flour
1 cup heavy cream

Cut the lobster shells—the body, tail, claws, and 4 or 5 legs—into small pieces. Place the shells in the blender or work bowl and run the food processor for 2 minutes or more until the shell is pulverized. From time to time, if necessary, stop the food processor and scrape the sides of the container with a rubber spatula.

Melt 1 tablespoon of butter in a skillet. Add the shells and sauté over medium heat for 1 minute.

Pour on the cognac and ignite.

When the cognac is burned off, add the fish stock or chicken broth and cook for 2 minutes.

Strain the sauce through a very fine sieve or two layers of cheesecloth and return it to the skillet.

Using your hands, or your blender or work bowl, mix the flour with the remaining butter, blending until all the flour has been absorbed in the butter.

Keep a low heat under your skillet. Stirring constantly, add the *beurre manié* to the sauce. Cook, stirring all the while, for a minute or so, until the sauce thickens. Taste and correct the seasonings.

Remove from heat, and, just before serving, gradually stir the cream into the sauce.

Pour the Coulis Sauce into a sauceboat and serve with the crepes.

COLD SOLE MOUSSE
(BLENDER OR STEEL BLADE; SLICING BLADE, IF DESIRED;
WHISK ATTACHMENT OR HAND BEATER)

This chilled fish mousse is especially good when accompanied by a hot Salsa Verde (see page 190), redolent with fresh parsley. We give instructions below for decorating a 1½-quart round mold, but if you have a fish mold, use that, creating an eye with a slice of egg or lemon and fins with a branch of watercress. If you wish, you can replace the sole with flounder, haddock, or cod.

Ingredients

1 pound fillet of sole
1 small onion
2 sprigs parsley
1 cup clam juice
1 egg white
1 envelope unflavored gelatin

1 hard-boiled egg for
    decoration
Salt and pepper to taste
1 cup mayonnaise (see
    page 177)
1 cup heavy cream
Watercress for decoration

Prepare the aspic and decorate the mold:

Slice the onion, either by hand or, if desired, using the slicing blade.

Place the onion, parsley sprigs, and clam juice in a saucepan.

Beat the egg white lightly with a fork and add to the saucepan. Bring the liquid to a boil, lower the heat, and simmer for 10 minutes.

Remove the saucepan from the heat and let stand for 15 minutes. When the liquid reaches room temperature, strain through a fine sieve or a layer of cheesecloth into a bowl.

Meanwhile, in a small bowl, soften the gelatin with 2 tablespoons of cold water. Place the bowl in a pan of simmering water and stir until the gelatin is completely dissolved.

Add the gelatin to the broth and mix well.

Rinse a 1½-quart mold under cold water. Cover the bottom of the mold with a layer of the cool but still liquid aspic. Chill in the freezer for 5 minutes until the aspic sets.

Using a grapefruit knife or the tip of a spoon, cut daisy petals out of the hard-boiled egg white. In the center of the bottom of the mold, arrange the daisy petals. Cut a small piece of yolk and place it in the center. With several sprigs of watercress, make a stalk and leaves (see illustration above).

Using a teaspoon, pour a few drops of the liquid aspic over the decorations to coat them. Reserve the remaining aspic, but do not refrigerate.

Chill the mold in the refrigerator until ready to fill.

Prepare the fish mousse:

In a skillet, season the fish with salt and pepper to taste. Cover the fillets with 1 cup of boiling water and simmer for about 15 minutes until the fish flakes easily when tested with a fork.

Drain the cooked fillets and place in the blender or work bowl.

Add the reserved aspic and the mayonnaise and run the food processor for 2 minutes; transfer the mixture to a bowl.

Beat the heavy cream until stiff using the whisk attachment or a hand beater.

With a wooden spoon, gently fold the beaten cream into the fish.

Retrieve the decorated mold from the refrigerator and pour the fish mousse into it. Cover with waxed paper and chill for several hours, preferably overnight.

At serving time, unmold the mousse onto a platter decorated with watercress. To loosen the mousse, dip the mold quickly into a bowl filled with hot water.

Accompany the mousse with a sauceboat filled with heated Salsa Verde and serve with a very cold, dry white wine.

Yield: 6 servings

Sauces

Hollandaise Sauces

These rich, foamy yellow sauces, when prepared by hand, can render even the most experienced cook nervous. Made by incorporating butter into egg yolks with no flour or similar substance to bind them, Hollandaise Sauces, until recently, were risky to prepare and fleeting once made: if heated too hot, the sauce would curdle; if allowed to cool, it would separate, and that was that. Now, we have discovered that with the food processor you can make a no-fail Hollandaise. What's more, the sauce need not separate, even when chilled, and will keep in the refrigerator for more than a week! The Hollandaise, Béarnaise, Choron, and Mousseline Sauces that follow are as light and delectable as ever.

HOLLANDAISE SAUCE
(BLENDER OR STEEL OR PLASTIC BLADE)

Ingredients

1 stick butter
3 egg yolks
2 tablespoons lemon juice

¼ teaspoon salt
Pepper to taste
Dash of cayenne

In a saucepan, melt the butter until it begins to bubble.
Place the egg yolks and the lemon juice in the blender or work bowl and run the food processor for 5 seconds. Stop the motor to

scrape the sides, if necessary. Run the food processor 2 seconds more.

With the food processor running, pour the butter through the feed tube in a very thin stream until all the butter has been incorporated.

Add a bit more lemon juice if desired and run the food processor a fraction of a second to mix. Season with salt, pepper, and cayenne.

Serve lukewarm.

Yield: About 1 cup

Note: If making the sauce several hours ahead, set in a pan of tepid water, and change the water from time to time. If you wish to make the sauce far ahead, or to save some of it for a week or more, store it in a tightly sealed container in the refrigerator. Reheat in a double boiler or in a saucepan over a low flame, stirring constantly, until the sauce is tepid. Pour into a sauceboat and serve.

BÉARNAISE SAUCE
(BLENDER OR STEEL BLADE)

Ingredients

3 shallots
1 cup Hollandaise Sauce (see page 173)
2 tablespoons white wine

1 tablespoon tarragon vinegar
1 teaspoon dried tarragon
¼ teaspoon freshly ground pepper

Chop the shallots in the blender or work bowl; set aside.

Prepare the Hollandaise, omitting the lemon juice if desired; do not remove from the blender or work bowl.

In a saucepan, place the white wine, vinegar, chopped shallots, and tarragon. Cook over a high heat until almost all the liquid has boiled off, leaving only about 1 teaspoon.

Spoon the contents of the saucepan into the Hollandaise. Run the food processor for 2 seconds, or until mixed. Add the pepper. Serve lukewarm.

Yield: About 1 cup

CHORON SAUCE
(BLENDER OR STEEL OR PLASTIC BLADE)

Serve with broiled meats or fish.

Ingredients

1 cup Béarnaise Sauce (see page 174)

¼ cup tomato puree, fresh or canned

Prepare a Béarnaise Sauce in the blender or work bowl.

Add the tomato puree and run the food processor a fraction of a second, or just to mix.

Serve lukewarm.

Yield: 1¼ cups

MOUSSELINE SAUCE
(BLENDER OR STEEL OR PLASTIC BLADE; WHISK OR HAND BEATER)

A very light sauce for broccoli, asparagus, poached chicken, fish and fish mousses.

Ingredients

1 cup Hollandaise Sauce (see page 174)   **4 tablespoons heavy cream**

In the blender or work bowl, prepare a Hollandaise Sauce. Remove to a bowl and set in a pan of tepid water.

Using the mixing bowl set with the whisk attachment or a hand beater, beat the cream until it holds its peaks but is still bubbly.

Just before serving, with a rubber spatula fold the whipped cream gently into the Hollandaise.

Yield: 1½ cups

Mayonnaises

Homemade mayonnaise, infinitely better than store-bought, has a slightly piquant flavor, and is thick and pale yellow in color. Like a Hollandaise Sauce, a mayonnaise is an egg sauce, but this time oil, rather than butter, is incorporated into beaten egg yolks. To achieve the delicate balance needed to add the liquid without breaking down the eggs, we recommend following the instructions below and these simple rules. (1) Until the mixture becomes thick, pour the oil very slowly, in a very thin stream, through the feed tube; and (2) once you have started, do not stop running the food processor until half the oil has been added.

MAYONNAISE
(BLENDER OR STEEL OR PLASTIC BLADE)

This thick sauce, frequently called for in salads, fish mousses, and many aspics, is especially good with cold meats and chicken.

Ingredients

2 egg yolks

2 cups olive oil or vegetable oil

Juice of 1 lemon

Salt and pepper to taste

Place the egg yolks in the blender or work bowl and run the food processor for 4 seconds, or until the eggs are frothy.

With the food processor running, start pouring the oil in a very, very thin stream through the feed tube.

When the mixture seems to thicken, keep the food processor running but stop pouring the oil for 5 seconds. Then start again, first in a thin stream, then a bit faster, until 1 cup has been incorporated.

Stop the food processor and check that the sauce is thick and pale. If not, see Note below.

Start the food processor and, in a slow stream, add the lemon juice through the feed tube.

Continue running the food processor and add the remaining oil in a steady stream.

When all the oil has been added, remove the mayonnaise to a bowl. Season with salt and pepper to taste and, if desired, a bit more lemon juice. Mix well.

Chill well before serving. Mayonnaise, if stored in a tightly sealed container, will keep for a week or more in the refrigerator.

Yield: 3 cups

Note: If at this point or later, the mixture seems to be a liquid or the yolks appear to be separating from the oil, pour the mixture into a measuring cup.

Rinse off the blender or work bowl and blade and start again. Add a fresh yolk to the blender or work bowl, or 2 yolks if your food processor will not beat one, and run the food processor for 4 seconds, or until frothy.

Then, slowly, pour the mixture from the measuring cup through the feed tube, by droplets at first, then in a slow, steady stream.

When you have used up all the mixture, switch to oil, following the instructions above.

Add an additional cup of oil, in a steady stream, for each additional egg yolk.

MAYONNAISE COLLÉ
(BLENDER OR STEEL OR PLASTIC BLADE)

This sauce gives a shiny aspic finish, without the use of a mold, to hard-boiled eggs, sliced chicken breasts, or a whole poached fish. Mayonnaise Collé is perfect for dressing up a cold buffet: spread the sauce, while still soft, over any dish to be decorated; with a pastry bag pipe on frills; draw fins and such with a wooden spatula; then set the dish in the refrigerator for 15 minutes or more until the jellied sauce hardens.

Ingredients

2 cups mayonnaise (see page 177)
3 tablespoons chicken stock or broth
1½ tablespoons white wine

1 tablespoon tarragon vinegar
2 tablespoons unflavored gelatin
Salt and pepper to taste

In the top of a double boiler or in a small bowl, mix the chicken stock or broth, the white wine, and the vinegar. Add the gelatin and stir.

Set the mixture over boiling water, stirring with a wooden spoon until the gelatin has completely dissolved.

Let the mixture cool to room temperature.

Add the gelatin mixture to the mayonnaise and mix well. Season with salt and pepper to taste.

Spread the Mayonnaise Collé while soft. Should it harden, set in a pan of tepid water and let it warm to room temperature.

Yield: 2½ cups

GREEN MAYONNAISE
(BLENDER OR STEEL BLADE)

Serve with boiled beef, cold meats, fish or eggs en gelée.

Ingredients

8 sprigs parsley
10 blades fresh chive
  (optional)
1 sprig dill, or ½ teaspoon
  dried dill

1 tablespoon dried tarragon
1 tablespoon dried chervil
2 cups mayonnaise (see
  page 177)
Salt and pepper to taste

Wash the fresh herbs and pat dry. Place in the blender or work bowl. Add the dried herbs and run the food processor for 15 seconds, or until chopped fine.

Add the chopped herbs to the mayonnaise and run the food processor for 2 seconds, or until well mixed.

Taste and correct the seasonings, adding salt and pepper as needed.

Place the Green Mayonnaise in a bowl, cover and chill in refrigerator for 2 hours before serving.

Yield: 2 cups

Variations: Prepare the Green Mayonnaise as above, adding 2 tablespoons of any of the following: pickles, capers, or anchovies.

SAUCE TARTARE
(BLENDER OR STEEL AND PLASTIC BLADE)

Serve with fish or any type of seafood.

Ingredients

1½ cups mayonnaise (see page 177)

2 cornichons or 1 small dill pickle, cut in pieces

4 shallots

2 anchovy fillets

1 tablespoon capers, drained

1 tablespoon chopped parsley

1 tablespoon dried tarragon

1 teaspoon lemon juice

1 tablespoon Dijon-style mustard

Few drops wine vinegar (optional)

Salt and pepper to taste

In the blender or work bowl, place the cornichons or the dill pickle cut in pieces, the shallots, anchovies, capers, parsley, and tarragon. Run the food processor for 5 seconds, or until finely chopped.

Add the mixture to the mayonnaise. Mix well with the plastic blade or a wooden spoon.

Add the lemon juice, mustard, and, if you desire a strong sauce, a few drops of wine vinegar. Mix again.

Season with salt and pepper to taste. Correct the seasonings.

Chill before serving.

Yield: 1¾ cups

AÏOLI

(BLENDER OR STEEL BLADE)

This garlic mayonnaise, excellent with cold meats, boiled beef, poached chicken, or spread on baked French bread to accompany a bowl of hearty soup, is very strong; a little goes a long way.

Ingredients

1 thick slice good white bread, crusts removed
3 tablespoons milk
4 garlic cloves, peeled

2 egg yolks
1 cup olive oil
2 tablespoons lemon juice
Salt and pepper to taste

Set the bread in a bowl with the milk. Let soak for 10 minutes. Squeeze the bread to get all the milk out.

Place the bread and the garlic cloves in the blender or work bowl. Run the food processor 10 seconds, or until the mixture forms a paste.

With the food processor running, drop the egg yolks through the feed tube. Run for 10 seconds, or until the egg mixture is thick.

Without stopping the food processor, start adding the oil through the feed tube, very slowly at first, then in a slow, steady stream. Continue until all the oil has been added; the mixture should be thick and creamy.

Add the lemon juice through the feed tube and run the food processor for a few seconds to mix.

Remove the Aïoli to a bowl. Season with salt and pepper to taste and correct the seasonings, adding more lemon juice if desired.

Yield: About 2 cups

Béchamels and Other White Sauces

All white sauces begin with a roux to which a liquid—be it milk, cream, or a stock—is added. The principal white sauce, the one on which almost all the others build, is the Béchamel, made with milk; the same sauce made with a stock is a Velouté. The addition of other ingredients—egg yolks and butter for richness; bits of cheese for a golden-crusted gratinée; spices, mushrooms, leeks, and onions for added flavor and color—enhance the sauces and give them their various names, *but* the process is always the same: the flour is cooked and the liquid incorporated into it. For guidelines in preparing any of the white sauces, refer to the instructions given for the Béchamel Sauce. Below, we offer a handful of sauces, each a bit richer and more elaborate than the one before.

BÉCHAMEL SAUCE
(BLENDER OR STEEL OR PLASTIC BLADE)

This is the basic white sauce, made with milk or, sometimes, with cream. With a bit of salt and pepper added, and a spice, if you like, a Béchamel can be poured over boiled beef, poached chicken, or vegetables. When mixed with noodles or other pasta, or when spooned over a meat or vegetable to be gratinéed, a Béchamel is always sprinkled with cheese. The instructions below are standard for all the other white sauces; please refer to them as needed.

Ingredients

2 tablespoons butter	Salt and pepper to taste
3 tablespoons flour	1 teaspoon brandy (optional)
2½ cups milk	

In a saucepan, melt the butter.

When the butter is hot, add the flour *all at once* and start stirring with a wooden spoon.

Cook the roux slowly over a low flame, stirring all the while, until the flour has been absorbed by the butter and the mixture no longer sticks to the sides of the saucepan. This will take between 2 and 3 minutes.

Place the roux in the blender or work bowl and run the food processor for 2 seconds.

With the food processor running, pour the milk through the feed tube, very slowly at first, then in a steady stream.

Return the sauce to the saucepan and bring slowly to a boil, stirring all the while.

Turn the flame very low and simmer, stirring frequently, for about 15 minutes until the sauce is thick and smooth.

Season with salt and pepper to taste. Add brandy if desired.

Taste and correct seasonings.

If preparing in advance, cut a round of waxed paper, butter it, and place directly on the surface of the sauce to prevent a skin from forming.

Yield: About 2½ cups

MORNAY SAUCE
(BLENDER OR STEEL BLADE)

Serve with fish, poultry, eggs, noodles, vegetables, or any dish to be gratinéed.

Ingredients

2 tablespoons grated Gruyère
  or Swiss cheese
2 cups Béchamel Sauce (see
  page 182)

3 egg yolks
2 tablespoons butter

Grate the cheese very fine. Set aside.

Pour the Béchamel into the blender or work bowl. Add the yolks and run the food processor until well mixed, about 10 seconds.

Place the sauce in a saucepan and heat slowly, stirring frequently with a wooden spoon.

Over a low flame, add the butter to the sauce, stirring constantly until the butter has melted.

Add the grated cheese and stir. Taste and correct the seasonings.

Yield: 2½ cups

SAUCE VELOUTÉ
(BLENDER OR STEEL OR PLASTIC BLADE)

Serve Velouté, a white sauce made with stock instead of milk, with chicken or veal.

Prepare as you would a Béchamel, (see page 182) but, in place of milk, add 2½ cups of chicken stock to the roux.

Optional: Sauté 2 tablespoons of chopped onions and/or 2 tablespoons of chopped mushrooms in butter. Add to the simmering Velouté.

For a richer sauce: Beat ½ cup of cream and 2 egg yolks together. After adding the stock, continue running the food processor and slowly pour the cream-and-egg mixture through the feed tube in a thin stream.

Yield: About 2½ cups

SAUCE SUPRÈME
(BLENDER OR STEEL BLADE)

Serve with beef or chicken, with filled puff pastry shells or, with cheese added, to any dish to be gratinéed.

Ingredients

1 cup Sauce Velouté (see page 184)
3 mushrooms
2 cups chicken stock

1 cup heavy cream
Salt and pepper to taste
Pinch of cayenne

Prepare a Sauce Velouté.

Meanwhile, wash and trim the mushrooms. Slice thin, using a knife or, if desired, your slicing blade.

In a saucepan, heat the chicken stock.

Add the sliced mushrooms to the stock and bring to a boil. Boil rapidly until the stock is reduced to two thirds of a cup.

Lower the heat and stir the Sauce Velouté into the stock.

Cook slowly, over a low heat, until the sauce is reduced to 1 cup.

Remove from heat and season with salt and pepper to taste and cayenne.

Yield: 1 cup

BRETONNE SAUCE
(BLENDER OR STEEL BLADE)

Serve with fish, shellfish, or chicken.

Ingredients

1 cup Béchamel Sauce (see
   page 182)
1 leek, white part only
1 celery stalk, trimmed
1 small onion

3 tablespoons butter
¼ cup fish stock or chicken
   stock
Salt and pepper to taste

Place the vegetables in the blender or work bowl and run the food processor 5 seconds, or until very finely chopped.

Melt 2 tablespoons of butter in a skillet. When the butter is hot, add the vegetables and sauté until they are cooked but not brown, about 5 minutes.

Reheat the Béchamel Sauce, if necessary, stirring all the while.

Add the vegetables to the sauce.

Add the fish stock or the chicken stock and mix well.

Heat the sauce through.

Season with salt and pepper to taste. Correct the seasonings.

Just before serving, swirl in 1 tablespoon of butter.

Yield: 1½ cups

BÉCHAMEL WITH PAPRIKA
(BLENDER OR STEEL BLADE)

Serve with veal, chicken, eggs, fish, or hot hors d'oeuvres.

Ingredients

1 cup Béchamel Sauce (see
    page 182)*
1 tablespoon chopped onion

2 tablespoons paprika
1 tablespoon butter
Salt and pepper to taste

Add the chopped onion to a saucepan of water. Bring to a boil and drain the onion at once.

When you have finished simmering the Béchamel, add the onion and the paprika.

Taste and correct the seasonings, adding salt and pepper if necessary.

Just before serving, heat the sauce through.

Swirl in 1 tablespoon of butter at the last minute.

Yield: 1¼ cups

* When serving a Paprika Sauce with a veal, chicken, or fish mousse, prepare the Béchamel with cream instead of milk.

PESTO SAUCE
(BLENDER OR STEEL BLADE)

This lively sauce, made by grinding basil and nuts into a paste, needs no cooking and is sublime when tossed with a pat of butter over a steaming bowl of spaghetti. Since the sauce is simple yet versatile, pesto inspires variation: it can be heated until it is luke- warm, then poured over fresh vegetables, cold fish or fish mousse;

it can be spooned into soup; or, when mixed with bread crumbs, it can be used to baste chicken, broiled fish, or tomatoes. Though pesto is at its best in the summertime, when fresh basil is tender and abundant, it freezes remarkably well. To freeze, prepare the sauce without cheese and store in small, tightly sealed containers.

Ingredients

½ cup freshly grated Parmesan
  cheese*
1 cup fresh basil leaves
¼ cup pine nuts, walnuts, or
  pistachios

2 garlic cloves, peeled
Small bunch of parsley or a few
  sprigs arugula (optional)
¼ to ½ cup olive oil
Salt and pepper to taste

In the blender or work bowl, add the grated Parmesan, basil, nuts, garlic cloves, parsley or arugula, and oil. Run the food processor 15 seconds, or until the basil is finely chopped.

If the mixture seems too thick, add more oil or hot water, if desired, and run the food processor just to mix. Add salt and pepper to taste.

Serve cold or lukewarm.

Yield: About 2 cups

* Omit the cheese if you are preparing for freezing or if you plan to serve over fish.

TOMATO SAUCE
(SLICING BLADE; BLENDER OR STEEL BLADE)

This classic northern Italian sauce, at home over pasta, meat loaf, or stuffed vegetables, can be used whenever a subtle tomato sauce is called for. It is lovely as is or with sausages, mushrooms, oregano, or extra basil added. When fresh tomatoes are plentiful, we like to make up a large supply to freeze for the cold months ahead.

Ingredients

1 medium onion	2 parsley sprigs
1 celery stalk	4 basil leaves, or 1 teaspoon
2 medium carrots	dried basil
2½ pounds ripe tomatoes	Salt and pepper to taste
3 tablespoons olive oil	½ cup tomato paste
1 garlic clove	½ cup white wine or beef
	broth (optional)

Wash and trim vegetables.

Set the slicing blade in place. Fit the onion, celery, and carrots in the feed tube; push through to slice.

Meanwhile, quarter the tomatoes.

In a saucepan, heat the olive oil. Add the garlic clove and sauté until brown; with a slotted spoon remove the garlic and discard.

Add the tomatoes to the saucepan. Add the onions, celery, carrots, parsley, and basil. Season with salt and pepper to taste.

Cook over a medium heat for about 45 minutes, stirring frequently with a wooden spoon.

When the tomatoes have disintegrated, pour the sauce into the blender or work bowl. Run the food processor 20 seconds, or until the sauce is pureed.

Return the tomato sauce to the saucepan. Add the tomato paste and cook over medium heat for 5 minutes, stirring frequently. If the sauce seems too thick, add white wine or beef broth to thin it.

Season with salt and pepper to taste and serve.

Yield: About 3 cups

SALSA VERDE
(BLENDER OR STEEL BLADE)

Serve with any kind of cold seafood or fish mousse, with cold meats, or with steak tartare. In the wintertime, this sauce, poured over spaghetti and sprinkled with grated cheese, makes a fine substitute for a pesto.

Ingredients

1 cup spinach
12 sprigs parsley
1 garlic clove (optional)
1 cup olive oil

Salt and pepper to taste
Lemon juice to taste
  (optional)

Remove the stems from the spinach and parsley and wash well. Pat dry between paper towels.

Place the spinach, parsley, and garlic in the blender or work bowl. Run the food processor for 5 seconds. Stop and scrape the sides with a rubber spatula.

Run the food processor and pour the olive oil through the feed tube, until all the oil has been added and the sauce is well mixed.

Remove to a bowl. Season with salt and pepper and, if serving with fish, lemon juice to taste.

Chill well in the refrigerator. The sauce will keep for several weeks.

Yield: About 1½ cups

JUS LIÉ (QUICK BROWN SAUCE)

Though we rarely have the time to make a real brown sauce—and know of few individuals who do—we can always make a *jus lié*, a fine substitute when used as the base for other sauces. Pan juices from meat being roasted or broiled, added to *jus lié* and reduced, make good, simple gravies.

Ingredients

2 cups strong beef stock or
  bouillon

2 teaspoons cornstarch
3 tablespoons water

In a saucepan, bring the beef stock or bouillon to a boil. Reduce the heat and cook for 15 minutes.

Dissolve the cornstarch in the water.

When dissolved, add the cornstarch to the stock and cook, stirring, until the sauce thickens.

Yield: About 2½ cups

FINES HERBES SAUCE
(BLENDER OR STEEL BLADE)

Serve with any roast or broiled red meat.

Ingredients

1 cup brown sauce or *jus lié*
  (see page 191)
1 medium shallot
1 teaspoon dried tarragon
10 blades of chive, or
  1 teaspoon dried chives

½ cup white wine
2 tablespoons butter
Few drops lemon juice to taste
Salt and pepper to taste
Chopped parsley for garnish

Prepare the *jus lié* and keep warm.

Meanwhile, in the blender or work bowl, place the shallot, tarragon, chives, and white wine. Run the food processor for 5 seconds, or until the shallot is chopped fine.

Place the mixture in a saucepan and bring to a boil. Cook over a medium heat until the wine mixture is reduced by half.

Strain the liquid into the hot *jus lié.*

Heat the sauce, stirring.

Remove from heat; add butter, lemon juice, and salt and pepper to taste.

Pour the sauce into a sauceboat and, just before serving, sprinkle with chopped parsley.

Yield: 1¼ cups

LEMON CAPER SAUCE
(BLENDER OR STEEL BLADE)

Serve with poached or broiled fish, crabmeat, croquettes, asparagus, or broccoli.

Ingredients

¼ cup lemon juice
10 capers
1 stick butter, cut in small
   pieces

4 tablespoons chicken broth
Salt and pepper to taste

Place the lemon juice in a small saucepan and boil until it is reduced to 1 tablespoon.

Meanwhile, in the blender or work bowl, chop the capers fine; set aside.

Add the lemon juice to the blender or work bowl. Run the food processor and drop the butter, one piece at a time, through the feed tube.

When the mixture forms a paste, pour the chicken broth through the feed tube and continue running the food processor for 2 seconds.

Transfer the mixture to a bowl or a sauceboat. Add the chopped capers and season with salt and pepper to taste. Mix well and serve at room temperature.*

Yield: 1 cup

* The sauce can be stored in the refrigerator and served cold on broiled steaks.

SAUCE PIQUANTE
(BLENDER OR STEEL BLADE)

Serve with sweetbreads, roast chicken, or any red meat.

Ingredients

1 cup brown sauce or *jus lié*
  (see page 191)
1 medium shallot
2 cornichons or small sour
  gherkins
1 sprig parsley

10 blades of chive, or
  1 teaspoon dried chives
3 tablespoons white wine
1½ tablespoons wine vinegar
Salt and pepper to taste
Pinch of tarragon

In the blender or work bowl, chop the shallot fine; set aside.

Place the pickles, parsley sprig, and chives in the blender or work bowl. Run the food processor until the pickles are finely chopped. Remove to a bowl.

Add the wine, vinegar, and shallots to a saucepan and bring to a boil. Lower the heat slightly and cook until the liquid is reduced by half.

Pour in the *jus lié* and bring the sauce to a boil.

Remove from heat; add the chives, parsley, and cornichons. Mix well and season with salt and pepper to taste.

Just before serving, spinkle the sauce with a pinch of tarragon.

Yield: 1¼ cups

Vinaigrettes and
Other Dressings for Green Salads

CLASSIC VINAIGRETTE
(BLENDER OR STEEL OR PLASTIC BLADE)

Ingredients

2 tablespoons wine vinegar
6 tablespoons olive oil
½ teaspoon salt

½ teaspoon Dijon-style
   mustard (optional)
Freshly ground pepper to taste

Place all the ingredients in the blender or work bowl. Run the food processor for 3 seconds to mix thoroughly.

Pour over salad greens just before serving.

Yield: ½ cup

GARLIC VINAIGRETTE
(BLENDER OR STEEL BLADE)

Prepare the dressing above, but add 1 garlic clove.

Run the food processor about 10 seconds, or until the garlic is chopped fine.

HERBAL VINAIGRETTE
(BLENDER OR STEEL BLADE)

Ingredients

1 cup Vinaigrette (see page 195)   1 teaspoon dried tarragon
4 parsley sprigs, washed and   1 teaspoon dried or chopped
   dried   fresh chervil

Place all the ingredients in the blender or work bowl.
Run the food processor for 5 seconds, or until the parsley is chopped fine.

Yield: 1 cup

ROQUEFORT DRESSING
(BLENDER OR STEEL OR PLASTIC BLADE)

Ingredients

¼ cup vinegar   2 tablespoons heavy cream
½ cup olive oil   ¼ teaspoon pepper
¼ cup Roquefort cheese   ¼ teaspoon salt

Add all the ingredients to the blender or work bowl and run the food processor for 5 seconds.
Pour the dressing over the salad just before tossing.

Yield: About 1 cup

CHIFFONADE DRESSING
(BLENDER OR STEEL BLADE)

Pour over or use as a marinade for cooked leeks, sliced zucchini, cold sliced potatoes, or cauliflower. This is also a fine dressing for a watercress salad.

Ingredients

½ cup Vinaigrette (see page 195)
2 hard-boiled eggs
1 medium pickled beet

10 green olives, pitted
½ small onion
3 sprigs parsley or 1 teaspoon chopped parsley

Place the hard-boiled eggs in the blender or work bowl. Run the food processor for 2 seconds, or until chopped, but not too fine.

To the blender or work bowl, add the pickled beet, green olives, onion and parsley sprigs. Run the food processor about 5 seconds, or until finely chopped.

Add the Vinaigrette and run the food processor for a fraction of a second, just to mix.

Pour the dressing over the cooked vegetables or, at the last minute, over a watercress salad.

Yield: ¾ cup

VINAIGRETTE NORMANDY
(BLENDER OR STEEL BLADE)

Pour over a chicory or raw spinach salad.

Ingredients

3 bacon slices, cut in small
   pieces
2 tablespoons wine vinegar
¼ teaspoon salt

Freshly ground pepper to taste
¼ cup walnuts, coarsely
   chopped

Melt the bacon in a skillet until crisp. Reserve the fat and, with a slotted spoon, remove the bacon to a paper towel to drain.

In the blender or work bowl, place the vinegar, salt, and 6 tablespoons of hot bacon fat. Run the food processor 5 seconds, or until well mixed. Add pepper to taste.

Pour the dressing over chicory or raw spinach.

Sprinkle the salad with the chopped walnuts. Crumble the bacon on top. Serve at once.

Yield: About ½ cup

Variation: With the slicing blade, slice 1 cup of raw mushrooms. Add to the chicory or spinach for a larger, more filling salad; dress, toss, and serve.

Vegetables

ZUCCHINI PANCAKES
(SHREDDING BLADE; BLENDER OR STEEL BLADE)

Ingredients

2 pounds zucchini
½ cup flour
1 teaspoon baking powder
1 egg

Salt and pepper to taste
2 tablespoons oil
½ cup grated Parmesan cheese
4 tablespoons butter

Wash and dry the zucchini and cut off the ends. Cut the zucchini in 3 or 4 pieces and place in the blender or work bowl. Run the food processor for 30 seconds, or until zucchini is finely chopped.

Add the flour, baking powder, and egg; run the food processor for 5 seconds, or until mixed well.

Transfer to a bowl and season with pepper and lightly with salt; the Parmesan, to be sprinkled on later, is salty.*

In a large skillet or on a griddle, heat the oil. When it is hot, drop ¼ cup of batter for each pancake and press very lightly with a spatula.

Cook the pancakes on one side for about 4 minutes until they are brown; turn with a spatula and cook on the other side.

Melt the butter and pour into a sauceboat.

Serve the pancakes hot with the butter and Parmesan alongside.

Yield: 6 servings

---

* The batter can be prepared ahead and will keep in the refrigerator for 2 or 3 days.

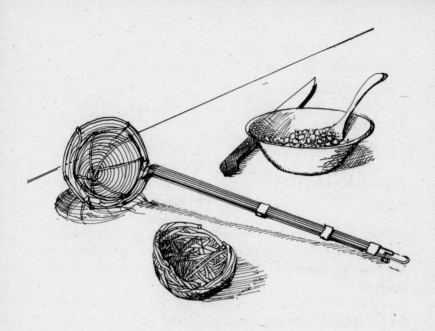

STRAW POTATO BASKETS WITH PEAS
(JULIENNE OR SHREDDING BLADE)

Julienne potatoes, crisply fried, are always delicious, but if you
have a Bird's-Nest Maker they can become elegant baskets to fill
with bright garden vegetables or tiny shrimp. Here, we fill nests of
potato with fresh peas, but you may want to try buttered baby
carrots or a chiffonade of spinach. If you do not own a Bird's-Nest
Maker, you can still deep-fry the straw potatoes and fashion a
beautiful platter, molding a mountain or dome in the center and
filling the surrounding valley with peas. To do this, invert a small
bowl in the center of a platter with raised edges. Shred the potatoes
and fry them, in deep fat, a few handfuls at a time, as you would
for plain juliennes. As each batch is cooked, spread the potatoes
over the platter and the bowl. Place the platter in a warm oven for

several minutes until the potatoes have set; then tilt gently and remove the bowl.

Ingredients

2 pounds baking potatoes
1 head Boston lettuce
2 pounds small fresh peas or
   2 packages frozen

4 tablespoons butter
2 cups chicken broth
Oil for deep frying
Salt and pepper to taste

Wash and peel the potatoes.

Wash the Boston lettuce, separating the leaves, and dry.

If fresh, shell the peas. If frozen, cook according to the directions on the package and drain.

In a saucepan, melt the butter. When hot, add the lettuce and cook over a low heat for about 6 minutes until the lettuce is soft but not wilted.

Add the peas and the chicken broth to the saucepan. Cook, over a medium heat, until the peas are tender, but do not overcook.

Keep warm while making the potato baskets.

Meanwhile, set the food processor with the julienne or shredding blade. Cut the potatoes to fit the feed tube and push through to shred. Rinse quickly in cold water.

Spread the potatoes between several layers of paper toweling for a few minutes to remove excess water; dry well.

In a deep fryer, heat the oil to 360°.

Lightly oil the Bird's-Nest Maker. Following the shape of the bottom, cover the bottom with julienne potatoes. Press the top of the Bird's-Nest Maker down and affix.

When the oil is hot, plunge the basket in and cook the potatoes until golden brown.

Remove the basket from the oil, wait a minute or so, remove the top, turn over, and gently tap the basket; the potatoes will fall out.

Place right-side up on an ovenproof platter in a very low oven— about 200°—while you make the rest of the potato baskets.

Repeat the process for each basket; salt lightly, if desired.

When ready to serve, reheat the peas, if necessary, and season with salt and pepper to taste.

With a slotted spoon, spoon the peas and lettuce into the baskets. Serve at once.

Yield: 6 servings

GINGERED YAMS
(BLENDER OR STEEL BLADE; SHREDDING BLADE)

1 pound yams or sweet
    potatoes, fresh or canned
⅔ cup sugar
1 tablespoon molasses
1 tablespoon brandy
1 teaspoon nutmeg
1 egg

1 stick plus 2 tablespoons
    butter
1 tangerine rind or orange rind,
    grated
Salt and pepper to taste
¼ pound fresh ginger
6 oranges to stuff (optional)
1 tablespoon brown sugar

Preheat the oven to 450°.

Boil the yams until tender; drain and peel. If using canned yams or sweet potatoes, drain well.

Cut the yams into several pieces and place in the blender or work bowl. Add the sugar, molasses, brandy, nutmeg, egg, and 1 stick of butter cut in small pieces. Run the food processor for 30 seconds.

Cut a tangerine rind or an orange rind into several pieces and add to the blender or work bowl. Run the food processor for 15 seconds, or until the peel is chopped fine.

Remove the potatoes to a bowl. Season with salt and pepper to taste.

Set the shredding blade in place. Peel the ginger and fit in the feed tube; push through to grate.

Add the ginger to the yam mixture, reserving a teaspoon to sprinkle on top.

Pour the yams into a 1½-quart baking dish or, if stuffing the oranges, cut off the top third and remove the pulp, reserving it for another use. Spoon the yam mixture into the shells and set the oranges in a shallow baking dish.

Sprinkle the reserved ginger over the yams. Top with brown sugar and dot with the remaining butter.

Place in a preheated 450° oven for 20 to 25 minutes, until the brown sugar melts and the potatoes are heated through.

Yield: 6 servings

ESCAROLE WITH LEMON SAUCE
(SLICING BLADE; BLENDER OR STEEL OR PLASTIC BLADE)

Ingredients

1 head escarole	½ teaspoon salt
3 cups chicken stock or broth	Pepper to taste
⅓ cup lemon juice	2 egg yolks
3 tablespoons butter	

Wash the escarole and separate the leaves. Drain and dry well.

Set the slicing blade in place. For long thin shreds, drop the escarole, leaf by leaf, through the feed tube, pushing as necessary.

In a saucepan, place the chicken stock or broth, the lemon juice, butter, salt, and pepper. Bring to a boil.

Add the escarole and cook, covered, over a high heat for 4 or 5 minutes.

With a large slotted spoon, remove the escarole to a bowl and keep warm on the side of the stove.

Reduce the lemon juice and broth to 1 cup.

In the blender or work bowl, place the 2 egg yolks and beat for several seconds until frothy.

Slowly, with the food processor running, add 3 tablespoons of the broth. Continue running and add the remaining broth in a steady stream, until the sauce resembles a very thin mayonnaise.

Pour the sauce over the escarole to coat it lightly. Serve at once.

Yield: 6 servings

FRIED POTATO PUFFS WITH CHEESE
(BLENDER OR STEEL BLADE)

Ingredients

3 pounds baking potatoes
1 cup bread crumbs made from
   good white bread
3 whole eggs
3 egg yolks
3 tablespoons butter
2 tablespoons grated Gruyère
   cheese

¼ teaspoon nutmeg
1 teaspoon salt
Pepper to taste
1 tablespoon peanut or
   vegetable oil
Oil for deep frying
3 tablespoons chopped parsley

Preheat the oven to 425°.

Scrub the potatoes and bake in a hot oven for 45 minutes to an hour, until tender when pierced with a fork.

Meanwhile, if necessary, prepare and set aside the grated cheese, bread crumbs, and parsley.

When the potatoes are cooked, scoop out the meat and discard the skins.

Place the potato pulps in the blender or work bowl.

Add 2 whole eggs and 3 yolks to the potatoes. Add the butter, grated cheese, nutmeg, and salt and pepper. Run the food processor for 15 seconds, or until mixed well. Remove to a bowl.

With your hands, shape the potatoes into fingers or cylinders, about 2 inches long and ½ inch thick.

In a dish, beat the remaining egg with 1 tablespoon of oil.

Roll the potatoes first in the beaten egg, then in the bread crumbs until well coated.

In a deep fryer, heat the frying oil to 375°. Add the potatoes and fry until golden brown.

Sprinkle the potato puffs with chopped parsley and serve at once.

Yield: 6 servings

ARTICHOKE PUREE
(BLENDER OR STEEL BLADE)

This unusual, high cuisine dish, which can be served in place of potatoes, is one to save for a very special occasion. The delicate light-as-air puree, made from a bountiful supply of artichoke bottoms, serves only four. It is splendid with broiled meats, and quite beautiful heaped high and sprinkled with nuts.

Ingredients

½ cup shelled pistachio nuts
3 12-ounce cans of artichoke
  bottoms, drained
1 cup heavy cream

1 teaspoon savory
Salt and pepper to taste
2 tablespoons butter

Plunge pistachio nuts for a few seconds in boiling water. Drain immediately and remove the skins.

Place the nuts in the blender or work bowl and chop fine, about 10 seconds. Remove to a bowl.

Drain the artichoke bottoms and cut in two.

In the blender or work bowl, place the artichoke bottoms, the cream, savory, and salt and pepper. Run the food processor for 45 seconds to puree.

In a saucepan, melt the butter. When it is hot, add the artichokes and heat slowly, over very low heat, stirring constantly.*

When the puree is heated through, arrange it in a mound in a warm bowl and cover with the chopped pistachio nuts.

Yield: 4 servings

* The dish may be prepared several hours ahead to this point and reheated in a double boiler.

PUREED SORREL
(BLENDER OR STEEL BLADE)

Ingredients

3 pounds sorrel, washed
3 tablespoons butter
2 tablespoons flour
1 teaspoon sugar

1 cup chicken broth
Salt and pepper to taste
2 egg yolks
½ cup heavy cream

Wash the sorrel well and remove some of the larger stems. Drain and pat dry.

Place the sorrel in a saucepan. Add 1 cup of water and cook, over a medium heat, until the sorrel has wilted, 5 to 8 minutes.

Drain and press the leaves with your hands to squeeze out the water.

Melt the butter in a saucepan and add the flour; mix well. Over a low heat, stirring constantly with a wooden spoon, cook the roux until the flour turns golden.

Still stirring, add the sorrel, sugar, chicken broth, and salt and pepper to taste. Cover the saucepan and cook over a medium flame for 15 minutes, stirring from time to time.

Place the contents of the saucepan in the blender or work bowl. Run the food processor for 1 minute, or until the sorrel is pureed.*

Add the egg yolks and run the food processor for 5 seconds.

Transfer to a saucepan and heat the sorrel through but do not boil.

Just before serving, add the cream and stir with a wooden spoon. Serve at once.

Yield: 6 to 8 servings

* The sorrel can be prepared several hours ahead of time to this point.

PUREE OF CAULIFLOWER
(BLENDER OR STEEL BLADE)

Ingredients

1 medium head of cauliflower
1 egg
¼ cup heavy cream
4 tablespoons butter

¼ teaspoon nutmeg
Salt and pepper to taste
4 tablespoons grated Parmesan cheese

In a large saucepan, bring 4 cups of water with 1 teaspoon of salt to a boil.

Wash the cauliflower, remove the center core, and add the cauliflower to the saucepan. Boil rapidly until tender when pierced with a fork but do not overcook. Drain.

When the cauliflower is cool enough to handle, cut off and discard any thick stems.

Place the flowerets in the blender or work bowl. Add the egg, heavy cream, 2 tablespoons of butter, and nutmeg. Run the food processor for 1 minute, or until pureed.

Taste and season, adding pepper and only a bit of salt since the Parmesan is already salty.

Pour the cauliflower puree into a gratin dish.

Sprinkle the Parmesan on top. Dot with butter.*

Place under the broiler until the cheese turns golden brown. Serve at once.

Yield: 6 to 8 servings

* The dish can be prepared ahead to this point. If allowed to cool, set in a 350° oven and reheat for 10 minutes before placing under the broiler.

HOT POTATO SALAD
(SLICING BLADE; BLENDER OR STEEL BLADE)

Few aromas are more pleasing than that of olive oil heating on the stove. Here, just as the oil reaches the point of fragrance, we mix it with vinegar and pour it over warm, sliced new potatoes and fresh mussels. Though plenty of mussels is ideal, we generally add the number we feel like washing that day—1 quart is never a chore, but 2 quarts can be—and when we find small, firm new potatoes, we slice them, skin and all. The salad or vegetable, as you wish, is marvelous with cold meats and pâtés or broiled chicken.

Ingredients

1–2 quarts mussels
2 tablespoons butter
14 new or small boiling
  potatoes
3 scallions

⅔ cup olive oil
1 garlic clove (optional)
3 tablespoons wine vinegar
Salt and pepper to taste
Paprika

Preheat the oven to 325°.

Under cold running water, wash the mussels, scrape, and remove the beards.

In a kettle, melt the butter. Add the mussels and steam, covered, for 8 to 10 minutes until the shells open.

Drain, reserving the liquid. When the mussels are cool enough to handle, remove from the shell and place, with the broth, in the top of a double boiler or in a bowl over simmering water to keep warm and plump.

Meanwhile, scrub the potatoes well. Wash and trim the scallions.

Cover the potatoes with salted water and boil for about 20 minutes until tender but not soft.

Set the slicing blade in place. Drain the potatoes and fit in the feed tube; push through to slice.

Set the potatoes in a serving bowl in the oven. Turn off the heat.

Chop the scallions coarsely in the blender or work bowl.

In a small saucepan, heat the olive oil, with a garlic clove if desired.

When the oil is fragrant but not bubbling, add the vinegar, and salt and pepper to taste. Mix well.

With a slotted spoon, add the mussels to the potatoes. Toss lightly with a wooden spoon.

Pour the warm sauce over the salad.

Add the scallions and toss again. Sprinkle with paprika and serve at once.

Yield: 6 servings

SPINACH AND MUSHROOM SALAD
(SLICING BLADE; BLENDER OR STEEL BLADE)

½ pound fresh spinach
12 large, firm mushrooms
1 tablespoon butter
Salt and pepper to taste

1 cup Vinaigrette (see
  page 195)
1 teaspoon Dijon-style mustard
2 teaspoons grated onion
2 hard-boiled eggs

Wash the spinach well and drain. Pat between towels to remove excess moisture.

Wash and trim the mushrooms. Remove the stems and reserve. Dry well.

Set the slicing blade in place. Fit the spinach, a handful at a time, in the feed tube, and push through to shred. Remove to a salad bowl.*

Fit the mushroom caps in the feed tube and push through to slice. Add to the spinach.

Place the mushroom stems in the blender or work bowl. Run the food processor for about 3 seconds, or until finely chopped.

Melt the butter in the skillet. Add the chopped stems, sprinkle with salt and pepper to taste, and sauté for a minute. Set aside.

In the blender or work bowl, prepare the Vinaigrette. Add the Dijon mustard and the grated onion and run the food processor just to mix.

Pour the dressing over the spinach and mushroom salad and toss.

Slice the hard-boiled eggs and arrange them in a circle on top of the spinach.

Spoon some chopped mushroom stems and butter on each egg. Serve the salad at once.

Yield: 6 servings

* In the summertime, when spinach is young and the leaves small, we make this salad without shredding the spinach.

RAW CAULIFLOWER SALAD
(SLICING BLADE; STEEL BLADE OR BLENDER)

Ingredients

1 medium head cauliflower
1 head romaine lettuce
4 shallots
2 tablespoons wine vinegar

4 tablespoons olive oil
1 teaspoon Dijon-style mustard
Salt and pepper to taste
½ cup finely chopped parsley

Remove the center core from the cauliflower. Separate the flowerets, retaining 2 inches of stem.

Rinse under cold water and dry.

Meanwhile wash off the romaine, separate into leaves, and dry well.

Line the romaine leaves in a deep salad bowl so that, standing upright, they form both a border and a well for holding the cauliflower salad.

Set the slicing blade in place. One by one, drop a floweret into the feed tube and push through to slice; continue until all the cauliflower is sliced.

Heap the cauliflower into the salad bowl.

Place the shallots, vinegar, oil, mustard, and salt and pepper in the blender or work bowl. Run the food processor for about 3 seconds, or until the shallots are chopped.

Pour the dressing over the cauliflower and sprinkle with chopped parsley.

Chill in the refrigerator for 1 hour before serving.

Yield: 8 to 10 servings

LEEK AND HARD-BOILED EGG SALAD
(SLICING BLADE; BLENDER OR STEEL BLADE)

Ingredients

6 large leeks
1 teaspoon salt
2 teaspoons wine vinegar
8 teaspoons olive oil
½ teaspoon Dijon-style
  mustard

1 garlic clove, peeled
Salt and pepper to taste
3 hard-boiled eggs
Chopped parsley for garnish

Trim the ends of the leeks. Wash very well under cold running water, taking care to remove all the sand.

Set the slicing blade in place. Stand the leeks upright in the feed tube and push through to slice.

Bring 1 quart of water, with 1 teaspoon of salt, to a boil in a saucepan.

Add the leeks to the boiling water and lower the flame; simmer for 10 minutes, or until just tender. Drain and pat dry.

Arrange the leeks on a long shallow platter.

Add vinegar, oil, mustard, garlic, and salt and pepper to the blender or work bowl. Run the food processor for about 20 seconds until the garlic is chopped.

Pour the dressing over the warm leeks.

Chill in the refrigerator for several hours.

Before serving, slice the hard-boiled eggs and arrange them on the bed of leeks. Sprinkle with chopped parsley and serve.

Yield: 6 servings

Leftovers

COLD CHICKEN EN CROÛTE
(BLENDER OR STEEL BLADE)

Ingredients

2 medium carrots
1 large onion
1 envelope unflavored gelatin
1½–2 cups mayonnaise (see
   page 177)

2½ cups cooked chicken
2 tablespoons butter
2 tablespoons tarragon
Salt and pepper to taste
1 loaf Italian or French bread

Scrape the carrots and cut in several pieces. Peel and quarter the onion.

Place the carrots and the onion in the blender or work bowl. Run the food processor 15 seconds, or until very finely chopped.

In a small bowl, mix the gelatin with 1 tablespoon of water. Place over simmering water, stirring until the gelatin is dissolved. Add the gelatin to the mayonnaise and mix.

Cut the chicken in cubes and place in the work bowl or, in small batches, in the blender. Add the butter and run the food processor 30 seconds, or until diced fine; transfer to a bowl.

Add the onions, carrots, and tarragon to the diced chicken. Mix well.

Add the mayonnaise and mix.

Season with salt and pepper to taste. Correct the seasonings; the chicken should be rather peppery.

Cut the loaf of bread in half vertically.

With a tablespoon, hollow out the loaf, removing as much of the soft bread as possible.

Spoon the chicken mixture into the hollowed bread, pushing with the back of the spoon so as to fit all the mixture in the bread.

When both halves are filled, wrap the bread tightly in aluminum foil and place in the refrigerator overnight.

Serve the cold chicken en croûte sliced thin with drinks or as garniture for a platter of broiled game hens.

Yield: 8 to 10 light hors d'oeuvres servings

MOCK CHICKEN QUENELLES
WITH LEMON SAUCE
(MEAT GRINDER OR STEEL BLADE; BLENDER; WHISK ATTACHMENT OR HAND BEATER)

Quenelles

Ingredients

2 cups cooked chicken
2 tablespoons flour
1 whole egg
Salt and pepper to taste

2 egg whites
4 cups chicken broth or bouillon
Chopped parsley for garnish

Cube the chicken. Grind it fine using the meat grinder attachment; or chop for about 30 seconds until fine in the work bowl or, in small batches, in the blender.

Place the chopped chicken in a bowl. Add the flour, a whole egg, and salt and pepper. Mix well.

With the whisk attachment or a hand beater, beat the egg whites until very stiff.

Fold the whites, using a rubber spatula, into the chicken mixture.

In a large saucepan, bring the chicken broth to a boil. Lower the flame to a simmer.

With two soup spoons or serving spoons, shape the chicken mixture into a quenelle (see illustration at top of page 219).

Gently drop each quenelle into the simmering broth.

Continue making and poaching the quenelles until all the chicken mixture has been used.

Cook for about 10 minutes, or until the quenelle is light but firm.

As each quenelle is cooked, remove it with a slotted spoon to a heated platter. Keep the quenelles warm while making the sauce. When ready to serve, sprinkle with chopped parsley.

Lemon Sauce

2–3 cups chicken broth
3 tablespoons lemon juice
1 tablespoon tarragon

1 stick butter, cut in pieces
Salt and pepper to taste

Bring the remaining broth in the saucepan to a boil. Add the lemon juice and tarragon, and continue boiling until the liquid is reduced to 1 cup.

Pour the liquid into your blender or work bowl.

Start the food processor and add the butter through the feed tube, a tablespoon at a time. Run the food processor until the sauce is creamy.

Season the sauce with salt and pepper to taste. Serve in a sauceboat alongside the quenelles.

Yield: 6 servings

PARMENTIER
(MEAT GRINDER AND BLENDER OR STEEL BLADE; SLICING BLADE)

Ingredients

6 large boiling potatoes
1 pound cooked beef or lamb
1 medium onion, quartered
3 tablespoons butter
2 cups cooked beans or peas
   (optional)

Salt and pepper to taste
½ cup milk or cream
1 egg
4 ounces Gruyère or Swiss
   cheese

Preheat the oven to 350°.

Peel the potatoes, quarter, and boil in salted water for 20 minutes, or until tender. Drain.

Cut the meat into cubes. Grind in the meat grinder attachment or chop for about 15 seconds in the work bowl. Remove to a bowl.

In the blender or work bowl, chop the onion for 4 seconds.

Melt 1 tablespoon of butter in a skillet. When the butter is hot, add the onion and sauté until golden brown.

Add the onion and, if desired, the leftover beans or peas to the ground meat. Mix lightly and season with salt and pepper to taste.

Place the boiled potatoes in the blender or work bowl. Add the milk or cream and run the food processor until the potatoes are pureed, about 15 seconds.

Add the egg and salt and pepper to taste to the puree. Run the food processor 5 seconds.

Cover the bottom of a gratin pan with the ground meat mixture. Spread the potato puree on top to cover.

Set the slicing blade in place. Fit the cheese into the feed tube and push through for small, thin slices.

Sprinkle the potatoes with the cheese slices.

Dot the potatoes and cheese with the remaining butter.

Place on a baking sheet in a preheated 350° oven. Bake for 20 minutes, or until the cheese melts to form a golden brown crust.

Serve piping hot with a crisp green salad.

Yield: 6 to 8 servings

STUFFED EGGS À LA COQUE
(BLENDER AND MEAT GRINDER OR STEEL BLADE)

Ingredients

6 whole eggs
1 cup cooked ham, pork, or
    chicken
2 tablespoons fresh bread
    crumbs
3 scallions, washed and
    trimmed

1 tablespoon sesame oil
    (available in Oriental food
    shops)
Salt and pepper to taste
Chopped parsley for decoration

With a straight pin, pierce each end of 6 eggs. Chip away at the top pinhole until you have an opening about the size of a dime.

Over a small bowl, hold one egg to your mouth. Blow through the small pinhole until the raw egg comes bursting out; set this first egg aside.

Over a larger bowl, blow the remaining eggs, reserving the raw eggs for another use.

Set the 6 eggshells safely aside so that they can be stuffed later on.

Use the blender or work bowl to chop the scallions, including the green part, and, if necessary, the parsley and bread crumbs. Set aside.

Cut the meat into cubes and chop, using the meat grinder, the steel blade, or, in small batches, the blender.

In a bowl, mix the meat, scallion, 1 egg, and sesame oil together. Season with salt and pepper to taste.

Add the bread crumbs and mix again.

Using a demitasse spoon, fill the empty shells with the meat mixture.

Securely cover the top of each egg with aluminum foil.

Place the eggs in a steamer and steam, over boiling water, for 20 minutes.

Set the stuffed eggs in egg cups and remove the aluminum foil. Sprinkle chopped parsley over the meat mixture.

Serve the warm stuffed eggs in egg cups as a first course or, with a tomato salad, as a light meal.

Yield: 6 servings

STUFFED VINE LEAVES
(MEAT GRINDER AND BLENDER OR STEEL BLADE)

Ingredients

1-pound jar of vine or grape
    leaves, or six dozen loose
    leaves
1 pound lamb or beef
1 cup raw rice
½ cup chopped parsley
1 cup olive oil

½ cup fresh lemon juice
1 tablespoon cumin
Salt and pepper to taste
2 garlic cloves, peeled
2 cups chicken broth
1½ cups yogurt or tahini paste,
    if available (optional)

Preheat the oven to 375°.

Wash the vine leaves under cold running water to rinse off the brine. Place in a bowl, cover with boiling water, and let stand 5 minutes. Drain.

Cut the meat into cubes. Push through the meat grinder, or place in the work bowl and run the food processor until finely ground. Remove to a bowl.

To the meat, add the rice, the chopped parsley, ½ cup of olive oil, ¼ cup of lemon juice, cumin, and salt and pepper to taste; mix well. Taste and correct the seasonings.

Spread out the leaves. In the center of a vine leaf, place 1 table-spoon of the meat-and-rice stuffing. Fold the base of the leaf up and over the stuffing, fold the sides in, and roll the leaf tightly to make a cylinder about 2½ inches long and ½ to ¾ inch thick.

Fill and roll the vine leaves until you have used all the stuffing. Cover the bottom of a kettle with 3 or 4 loose vine leaves.

Place a layer of stuffed vine leaves, close together, seam side down along the bottom. Arrange another tightly packed layer on top of that, continuing until all the stuffed leaves have been added. Cover the stuffed vine leaves with 2 or 3 loose leaves.

Cut the garlic cloves into 2 or 3 pieces and sprinkle over the leaves.

Pour the remaining oil over.

Add chicken broth to cover.

Place the kettle, covered, in a preheated 375° oven and cook until the rice is done, about 35 minutes.

When cooked, arrange the grape leaves on a platter and pour the remaining lemon juice over. Serve hot or cold with yogurt or tahini paste or lemon wedges.

Yield: 30 to 50 stuffed vine leaves

CHICK PEA FRITTERS
(MEAT GRINDER AND BLENDER OR STEEL BLADE)

Ingredients

2 cups cooked lamb, beef, chicken, or turkey
1 cup parsley, tightly packed
1 large onion, peeled and quartered
1 cup fresh bread crumbs
1 pound cooked chick peas, or a 20-ounce can, drained

2 garlic cloves
1 teaspoon cumin
1 tablespoon butter
Salt and pepper to taste
1 egg
Lettuce for garnish, preferably Boston
Oil for deep frying

Chop the parsley and onion. Spread the bread crumbs over a dish so they can be used later for breading the fritters.

Cut the meat into cubes. Grind it, using the meat grinder attachment, or chop in the work bowl or, in small batches, in the blender.

Place the ground meat in the blender or work bowl. Add the chick peas, garlic cloves, and cumin. Run the food processor for 1 minute, or until chopped fine. Transfer to a bowl.

In a skillet, melt the butter. Add the chopped onions to the skillet and sauté until they are transparent but not brown. Add them to the chick pea mixture.

Add the chopped parsley to the mixture. Season with salt and pepper to taste, and mix well. Taste and correct the seasonings.

With your hands, roll the mixture into cylinders about 3 inches long and 1 inch in diameter.

In a bowl, beat the egg with 1 tablespoon of water.

Dip the chick pea fritters in the beaten egg, then roll in the bread crumbs until well coated. Continue until all the fritters are breaded.

In a deep fryer, heat the oil to 375°. When the oil is hot, fry 6 or 7 fritters at a time until golden brown.

Drain the fritters on paper towels and keep warm in a very low oven until all are cooked.

Cover a platter with lettuce leaves and arrange the fritters on top. Serve at once for a light meal or pass with drinks.

Yield: 30 fritters

PARISIAN PASTRY STICKS
(MEAT GRINDER OR STEEL BLADE; BLENDER)

Ingredients

Pâte brisée (see page 41)
½ cup chopped parsley
3 cups cooked brisket or
    pot roast
1 medium onion, quartered

1 tablespoon butter
3 tablespoons pot roast gravy
2 eggs
1 tablespoon tarragon
Salt and pepper to taste

Preheat the oven to 350°.

Make the pâte brisée, following the instructions, on page 41, *but* just before pouring in the ice water, add the chopped parsley and run the food processor for 5 seconds. Then pour in the ice water.

Roll the pâte brisée into a ball and set aside.

Chop the meat, using the meat grinder attachment, the steel blade, or, in small batches, the blender. Remove to a bowl.

Place the onion in the blender or work bowl. Run the food processor 3 seconds to chop.

In a skillet, melt the butter. When the butter is hot, add the onion and cook over a low heat until they are transparent and soft.

Add the onion to the meat. Add the gravy, 1 egg, the tarragon, and salt and pepper to taste. Mix thoroughly with a wooden spoon.

Taste the meat mixture and correct the seasonings.

Cut the dough ball in half.

On a floured board, with a floured rolling pin, roll each half into a rectangle about 12 inches long.

Cut the rectangles into 12-inch-long, 4-inch-wide strips.

Line the meat mixture, lengthwise, along the center of the dough. Continue until you have used up all the meat.

Fold the sides of the dough in toward the center to enclose the meat; the sticks should be about 2 inches wide. Seal the seams. Fold the ends in and seal.*

Place the sticks, seam side down, on a buttered baking sheet.

Beat the remaining egg lightly with 1 tablespoon of water.

Brush the stick with the beaten egg and place in a preheated 350° oven. Bake for about 25 minutes, or until golden brown.

Cut the sticks, on the diagonal, into 2-inch pieces.

Serve the freshly heated sticks with drinks or serve with a string bean salad for luncheon or dinner.

Yield: About 6 sticks

---

* Parisian pastry sticks may be prepared ahead to this point, wrapped tightly in aluminum foil, and frozen. They need not be defrosted before baking.

HOLIDAY TURKEY PIE

(PASTRY OR WHISK ATTACHMENT AND BLENDER OR STEEL BLADE)

Here, a flaky pie crust, a white sauce laced with cheese, and a sprinkling of herbs help you bid farewell to another holiday turkey. The instructions below are for a traditional-looking pie, slightly rounded in the center. However, if you own a wide cone-shaped pie top pan, now is the time to use it. The top and bottom crusts can be cooked together in a 350° oven for about 20 minutes; once the crust is filled, the previously cooked turkey meat need only be heated through. If you use the cone-shaped pan, butter it well and dust with flour before lining with dough, and take care when turning the top crust out of the pan and over the filling. Brush the top with beaten egg to glaze it and cook for about 10 minutes, or until golden brown. Serve with green beans, tossed with butter and garlic, and a chilled white wine.

The Dough

Ingredients

2 cups flour
¼ cup oil
¼ cup hot water

4 tablespoons butter, melted
1 egg
Extra flour and butter

The Turkey Filling

Ingredients

3 cups cooked turkey meat
¼ teaspoon sage
Salt and pepper to taste
1 cup Béchamel Sauce (see page 182)

Pinch of nutmeg or mace
½ cup Parmesan cheese, grated

[227]

Preheat the oven to 350°.

In the mixing bowl, set with the pastry or whisk attachment, or in the work bowl, place the flour, oil, hot water, and melted butter. Run the food processor for 1 minute, or until the dough forms a coarse meal.

Remove the dough and shape it into a ball. Dust the ball with flour and place in a bowl; let stand 15 or 20 minutes.

Meanwhile, cut the turkey meat into 1-inch cubes and place in a bowl. Season with sage, salt, and a bit heavily with pepper.

Make the Béchamel Sauce and season it with a pinch of nutmeg or mace. Taste and correct the seasonings.

Pour the Béchamel Sauce over the turkey meat and toss lightly with a wooden spoon. Sprinkle with grated cheese.

Taste the filling and correct the seasonings; set aside.

Butter a quiche pan or pie plate and dust with flour.

Cut the dough in half. On a floured board, with a floured rolling pin, roll half the dough to form the bottom crust.

Drape the dough over the pie plate, press the edges and prick the bottom several times with a fork.

Bake the pie shell in a preheated 350° oven for about 20 minutes, or until the dough is almost cooked.

Remove the bottom crust from the oven and spoon in the turkey filling.

Roll the remaining dough to form the top crust. Cover the pie and seal the edges.

Beat an egg with 1 tablespoon of water. Brush the top crust with the mixture.

Bake the turkey pie in a 350° oven for 15 to 20 minutes until the top is golden brown.

Yield: 6 servings

STUFFED POTATOES
(MEAT GRINDER AND BLENDER OR STEEL BLADE)

Ingredients

6 large boiling potatoes
2 cups cooked brisket or
  pot roast
6 scallions
Salt and pepper to taste

2 cups pot roast gravy
1 cup beef broth or bouillon,
  as needed
Chopped parsley for garnish

Peel the potatoes. Set in a bowl of cold water until ready to use.

Chop the meat, using the meat grinder attachment, the steel blade, or, in small batches, the blender; transfer to a bowl.

Wash and trim the scallions. Place the scallions, including the green part, in the blender or work bowl. Run the food processor 4 seconds to chop.

Mix the scallions in with the meat. Season the mixture with salt and pepper to taste.

Drain the potatoes. Cut a slice off the bottom so that each potato can stand upright.

Slice the top off each potato, about an inch down, and reserve the cap.

With a teaspoon, scoop out as much of the center flesh as possible.

Spoon the meat mixture into the hollowed potatoes.

Cover each potato with a reserved cap.

Stand the potatoes in a saucepan.

Pour in gravy and, if necessary, beef broth until the liquid reaches halfway up the potatoes.

Bring to a boil, lower the flame, and simmer for 25 minutes, or until the potatoes are cooked.

Arrange the potatoes on a small round platter, sprinkle with chopped parsley, and serve with an escarole salad.

Yield: 6 servings

STUFFED CABBAGE
(MEAT GRINDER AND BLENDER OR STEEL BLADE)

Ingredients

1 head cabbage
1 teaspoon salt
2 cups cooked pork, beef, lamb,
   or chicken
2 garlic cloves
1 teaspoon cumin
1 teaspoon sage

Salt and pepper to taste
¾ cup fresh bread crumbs
1 egg
4 slices of bacon
1 cup beef or chicken broth
1 cup yogurt
Chopped parsley for garnish

Remove the stem and as much of the center core as possible from the cabbage; discard any bruised outer leaves.

Place the cabbage and salt in a kettle. Fill with water and bring to a boil. Lower the heat and simmer for 25 minutes.

When the cabbage is just tender, refresh it under cold running water, separating the leaves. Set in a colander to drain.

Cut the meat into 1- or 1½-inch cubes. Grind with the meat grinder attachment, or place in the work bowl or, in small batches, in the blender, and run the food processor 15 seconds to chop.

In the blender or work bowl, season the ground meat with garlic cloves, cumin, sage, and salt and pepper to taste.

Add the bread crumbs and the egg and run the food processor for about 30 seconds, or until the ingredients are mixed well; the meat will be rather fine.

In the center of a cabbage leaf, place 1½ tablespoons of the meat mixture.

Fold the base of the leaf over once, fold in the sides, then roll the cabbage tightly around the stuffing.

Repeat until you have used up all the stuffing.

Cover the bottom of a saucepan with several loose cabbage leaves.

Starting at the outer edge, arrange the stuffed cabbage leaves in concentric circles until all have been placed in the saucepan.

Meanwhile, in a skillet cook the bacon slices until crisp.

Pour 1½ tablespoons of bacon fat over the cabbage. Drain the bacon slices on paper towels and crumble over the cabbage.

Add the beef or chicken broth to the saucepan, bring to a boil, then lower the flame and simmer covered for 25 minutes.

When the cabbage is cooked, pour out the pan juices without dislodging the cabbage. Strain the juices into a saucepan.

Place a plate over the cabbage and turn over carefully to remove the cabbage and the bottom leaves from the saucepan. Place a warm serving platter over the plate and invert once again so that the loose leaves are on the bottom holding the stuffed cabbage.

Add the yogurt to the pan juices and heat through, stirring, but do not boil. Pour into a sauceboat.

Sprinkle the stuffed cabbage with chopped parsley and serve with the yogurt sauce alongside.

Yield: 6 servings

FISH CROQUETTES WITH FUMET SAUCE

The Croquettes
(BLENDER OR STEEL BLADE)

Ingredients

2 cups cooked fish
½ cup fresh bread crumbs
3 eggs
2 tablespoons heavy cream

1 tablespoon tarragon
Salt and pepper to taste
Oil for deep frying

Pick over the cooked fish, discarding any bones and skin.

Place the fish in the blender or work bowl and run the food processor for 15 seconds.

To the fish, add 2 tablespoons of bread crumbs, 1 egg, the heavy cream, tarragon, and salt and pepper to taste. Run the food processor for 15 seconds. Taste and correct the seasonings, remove to a bowl.

In one dish, beat 2 eggs with 1 tablespoon of water.

In a second dish, spread the remaining bread crumbs.

Shape the fish mixture into cylinders 2 inches long and 1 inch in diameter.

Roll the croquettes first in beaten eggs, then in bread crumbs, until well coated.

Heat oil for deep frying. When the oil is hot, about 360°, add the fish croquettes, and cook until golden brown.

Drain on paper toweling and keep warm until serving time.

Serve the croquettes on a platter decorated with parsley sprigs. Accompany with Fumet Sauce.

Fumet Sauce

Ingredients

2 egg yolks   Pinch of cayenne
1 cup fish stock   Salt and pepper to taste
1 teaspoon lemon juice

Place the egg yolks in the blender or work bowl and run the food processor for 4 seconds, or until frothy.

With the food processor running, pour the fish stock through the feed tube, very slowly at first, then in a slow steady stream.

When all the stock has been added, pour the lemon juice through the feed tube and continue running the food processor until well mixed.

Pour the sauce into a bowl. Add cayenne, and salt and pepper to taste and mix well. Add more lemon juice, if desired.

Serve the warm sauce, in a bowl or sauceboat, alongside the fish croquettes.

Yield: 6 servings

FISH OR SHELLFISH SALAD
(BLENDER OR STEEL BLADE)

Ingredients

2 cups cooked fish or shellfish	1 teaspoon Dijon-style mustard
1 head romaine lettuce	Salt and pepper to taste
1 cup strong fish stock or	Pinch of nutmeg
clam juice	Few drops lemon juice
2 egg yolks	Several sprigs of dill

Pick over the fish or shellfish carefully, removing any skin, bones, or shell.

Wash the romaine, separating the leaves, and pat dry.

Line a deep salad bowl with the romaine leaves.

Spoon the fish or shellfish into the well in the center of the leaves and arrange in a mound.

Chill in the refrigerator until serving time.

Just before serving, heat the fish stock in a saucepan until warm.

Place the yolks and the mustard in the blender or work bowl and run the food processor for 4 seconds, or until the yolks are frothy.

With the food processor running, pour the warm stock, very slowly at first, then in a slow steady stream, through the feed tube.

[233]

Transfer the sauce to a bowl and season with salt and pepper to taste and nutmeg. Mix well.

Add lemon juice to taste and mix the sauce again.

At serving time, remove the salad from the refrigerator and pour the sauce over.

Snip the dill over the salad and serve.

Yield: 4 servings

Desserts

RESTON VIRGINIA BOURBON CAKE

(SHREDDING BLADE; WHISK ATTACHMENT OR STEEL OR PLASTIC BLADE;
HAND BEATER; FOLDING ATTACHMENT, IF AVAILABLE)

This fine cake is best served late on a Sunday afternoon or on a winter night with a pot of strong tea. Though we prefer baking this cake in a tube pan, a large loaf pan or two small ones will do nicely.

The Cake

Ingredients

2 orange rinds
2 cups confectioner's sugar
2 sticks butter, cut in small
pieces
5 eggs, separated

4 tablespoons bourbon
2¼ cups flour
1 teaspoon baking powder
½ teaspoon nutmeg
¼ teaspoon salt

Preheat the oven to 350°.

Set the shredding blade in place. Cut the orange rinds into pieces and fit into the feed tube; push through to grate. Set aside, reserving 2 tablespoons for the frosting.

Place the sugar and the butter cut in small pieces in the work bowl or in the mixing bowl set with the whisk attachment. Run the food processor for 20 seconds, or until the mixture is light and fluffy; remove to a bowl.

Place the egg yolks in the work bowl or mixing bowl and run the food processor for 15 seconds until the yolks are lemony yellow.

With the food processor running, add 2 tablespoons of bourbon and 2 tablespoons of grated orange rind.

Continue running the food processor and return the butter-sugar mixture to the blender or mixing bowl. Beat for 25 seconds, or until mixed well.

In another bowl, mix the flour, baking powder, nutmeg, and salt. Fold the flour mixture into the butter-and-sugar mixture.

Add 2 tablespoons more bourbon to the batter and set aside.

Place the egg whites with a pinch of salt in a clean mixing bowl and, with the whisk attachment or a hand beater, beat the whites until they hold peaks.

Using a rubber spatula or the whisk or folding attachment, gently fold the egg whites into the batter.

Butter a tube pan and pour the batter in.

Bake the cake in a preheated 350° oven for 1 hour, or until a straw inserted in the dough comes out clean.

Remove the cake from the oven and let stand for 10 minutes.

Unmold the cake and let cool for 10 minutes more before frosting.

The Frosting

Ingredients

1 stick butter, cut in small
 pieces
2 cups confectioner's sugar

3 tablespoons bourbon
2 tablespoons heavy cream

Meanwhile, in the work bowl or in the mixing bowl set with the whisk attachment, place the butter cut in small pieces, the confectioner's sugar, the bourbon, and the heavy cream. Run the food processor for about 15 seconds, or until the ingredients are thoroughly mixed.

While still warm, spread the frosting on the cake.

Sprinkle the reserved grated orange rind over the top of the cake.

Yield: 10 to 12 servings

DEEP CHOCOLATE CAKE
WITH HAZELNUTS
(SHREDDING BLADE; BLENDER OR STEEL BLADE; WHISK ATTACHMENT OR
HAND BEATER; FOLDING ATTACHMENT, IF AVAILABLE)

This very rich cake, the answer to a chocolate lover's dream, is best
when made a day or two in advance and stored in the refrigerator.
Slice quite thin, reassemble, and serve with a bowl of unsweetened
whipped cream alongside. Since one small piece goes a very long
way, this is the perfect cake for a champagne brunch as well as a
fine end to a large dinner party.

The Cake

Ingredients

2 cups hazelnuts, shelled
8 ounces unsweetened baking
    chocolate
¾ cup plus 4 teaspoons flour
1½ tablespoons baking powder
½ pound butter, cut in small
    pieces

1 cup plus 2 tablespoons very
    fine sugar
7 eggs
1 teaspoon vanilla extract
Pinch of salt
Butter for greasing the pans

Preheat the oven to 400°.

Place the hazelnuts in boiling water for 5 minutes to loosen the
skins; drain, and remove the skins.

On a buttered baking sheet, spread the nuts. Toast in a 400°
oven for 15 minutes, turning once or twice, until golden brown.
Remove the nuts from the oven and lower the heat to 275°.

Set the shredding blade in place. Fit the chocolate in the feed
tube and push through to grate; remove to a medium bowl.

In the blender or work bowl, place one cup of hazelnuts and run
the food processor until coarsely chopped. Remove to a small bowl
to sprinkle on the finished cake.

Add the remaining hazelnuts and run the food processor until they are pulverized. Pour the nuts into the bowl with the grated chocolate.

Add ¾ cup of flour and the baking powder to the chocolate and nuts; mix well.

Place butter, cut in small pieces, in the work bowl or in the mixing bowl set with the whisk attachment.

Add 1 cup of very fine sugar and .1 teaspoon of flour to the butter and run the food processor until the mixture is a smooth paste.

Separate the eggs, reserving the whites.

To the butter-flour mixture, with the food processor running, add the egg yolks, one at a time, waiting for each to be absorbed before adding the next.

Add the vanilla extract.

Now, with the food processor running, add the chocolate-and-flour mixture, a few tablespoons at a time, until all the ingredients are mixed in well.

In a clean mixing bowl, using a clean whisk or a hand beater, beat the egg whites, with a pinch of salt, until they are stiff.

Using a rubber spatula or the whisk or folding attachment, gently fold the whites into the batter.

Now grease an 8-inch cake pan with a pat of butter. Sprinkle the pan with 1 tablespoon of flour and tip the pan from side to side until evenly coated. Invert the pan to remove any excess flour.

Pour the batter into the cake pan.

Sprinkle 2 tablespoons of very fine sugar over the batter.

Place the cake in a preheated 275° oven and bake for 90 minutes, or until the sugar on top becomes crisp and forms a crust.

Remove the cake from the oven and let cool for 5 minutes.

After taking the cake out of the pan, let cool to room temperature before icing it.

The Icing

Ingredients

¾ cup sugar
7 ounces semisweet chocolate

1 tablespoon strong espresso
  coffee
⅓ cup water

Place the sugar, chocolate cut in small pieces, espresso, and water in the top of a double boiler or in a saucepan over a low heat. Cook, stirring all the while, until the mixture is smooth, taking care not to let the chocolate burn.

Let the icing cool for 10 minutes.

With a rubber spatula, spread the icing over the cake.

Sprinkle the reserved coarsely chopped hazelnuts over the top.

Serve the cake at room temperature with unsweetened whipped cream.

Yield: About 24 slices

GATEAU OF CREPES FILLED
WITH APRICOT SOUFFLÉ
(BLENDER OR STEEL BLADE; WHISK ATTACHMENT OR HAND BEATER;
FOLDING ATTACHMENT, IF AVAILABLE)

Crepe batter for 16 dessert
  crepes (see page 35)*
10 ounces dried apricots
4 egg yolks
1 cup plus 1 tablespoon sugar
½ cup heavy cream
2 tablespoons cornstarch
2 tablespoons cognac

5 egg whites
Pinch of salt
2 tablespoons confectioner's
  sugar
1 or 2 limes, cut in slices
Extra butter for crepe pan,
  pie plate

* When making the crepe batter, replace the salt with 1 teaspoon of sugar. Let stand for 1 hour.

Preheat the oven to 400°.

Place the dried apricots in a bowl, cover with hot water, and let stand for an hour or more.

Melt a pat of butter in a crepe pan. When the butter bubbles, pour in 3 tablespoons of batter, and quickly tilt and rotate the pan until the batter covers the entire surface.

Cook the crepes until they turn a very light tan, then turn with a spatula and cook for a few seconds on the other side. Slide the slightly undercooked crepes onto a plate.

Without rebuttering the pan, continue making slightly under-cooked crepes until you have used up all the batter. If you are not using them immediately, stack the crepes and cover with a damp cloth.*

Drain the apricots and place in the blender or work bowl. Add the egg yolks and 1 cup of sugar and run the food processor for 1 minute, or until the apricots are pureed.

Pour the cream through the feed tube and run the food processor for 5 seconds.

Dilute the cornstarch in the cognac. Add to the apricot puree and run the food processor for 5 seconds. Remove the mixture to a bowl.

In the mixing bowl set with the whisk attachment, or with a hand beater, beat the egg whites, with a pinch of salt, until they are very stiff.

Gently fold the apricots into the egg whites, using the whisk or folding attachment or a rubber spatula.

Butter a pie plate and place one crepe on the bottom. Cover the crepe with a layer of apricot soufflé about ½ inch thick. Place another crepe on top, cover with a layer of soufflé, and continue, alternating, until you have used up all the soufflé. Place a crepe on top so that the stack, when cooked, resembles a cake.

Sprinkle the top crepe with 1 tablespoon of sugar.

Place on a baking sheet in a preheated 400° oven and bake for

*The crepes may be prepared several hours in advance to this point.

[242]

20 minutes, or until the soufflé has risen and the top crepe is a golden brown.

Sprinkle the gateau with confectioner's sugar and serve at once. At the table, cut into wedges and offer each piece with a slice of lime.

Yield: 6 to 8 servings

MINCE PIE SERVED WITH STRAWBERRIES IN WHIPPED CREAM
(BLENDER OR STEEL BLADE; PASTRY OR WHISK ATTACHMENT OR STEEL BLADE; HAND BEATER)

The glory of this mince pie, a favorite over the holidays, is that the many mincemeats—plump and juicy from soaking in brandy and sherry for 3 to 4 days—retain their distinctive flavors since they cook for only a short time. The strawberries in whipped cream add a refreshing note between bites of this robust and delectable pie.

The Mincemeat

Ingredients

¼ pound fresh beef suet
¼ cup candied orange rind
¼ cup candied lemon rind
¼ cup almonds, shelled and skinned
½ pound apples
1 cup dried currants
2 cups seedless raisins

5 dried figs
½ teaspoon nutmeg
½ teaspoon allspice
½ teaspoon cinnamon
¼ teaspoon ground cloves
¾ cup sugar
1 cup brandy or cognac
½ cup dry sherry

[243]

Prepare the mincemeat 3 or 4 days ahead:

Place each of the following, separately, in the blender or work bowl and chop coarsely, about 4 to 5 seconds: the beef suet, candied orange rind, candied lemon rind. Transfer to a large bowl.

Place the almonds in the blender or work bowl and chop coarsely, about 10 seconds; add to the bowl.

Peel, quarter, and remove the core from the apples. Place in the blender or work bowl and run the food processor for 8 seconds; transfer to the bowl.

To the chopped suet, fruits, and nuts, add the currants, raisins, and the figs.

Sprinkle the mixture with nutmeg, allspice, cinnamon, and ground clove.

Add the sugar and mix well with a wooden spoon.

Pour the brandy and sherry over and toss with a wooden spoon until all the ingredients are moist.

Cover the bowl with a plate and set in a cool place—not the refrigerator—for 3 to 4 days until all the liquor has been absorbed.

The Pie Crust

Ingredients

1½ cups flour	9 tablespoons butter
3 tablespoons sugar	Extra flour and butter for the
2 eggs	pie plate

Preheat the oven to 375°.

In the work bowl, or in the mixing bowl set with the pastry or whisk attachment, place the flour, sugar, 1 egg, and butter cut in small pieces. Run the food processor for 15 seconds. Stop the machine and scrape the sides of the bowl.

Run the food processor for another 10 seconds, or until the dough clings together.

Shape the dough into a ball, dust with flour, and wrap in waxed paper. Chill in the refrigerator for 20 minutes.

Grease a 9-inch pie plate with butter and dust lightly with flour.

On a lightly floured board, roll two thirds of the dough to fit the pie plate.

Line the pan with the dough, trim the edges, and prick the bottom with a fork.

Bake the shell in a preheated 375° oven for 15 minutes, or until lightly browned.

Remove from the oven. Raise the oven heat to 400°.

Fill the pie shell with the mincement.

Roll the remaining dough to form the top crust, drape over the pie, and seal the edges.

Lightly beat 1 egg with 1 tablespoon of water and brush the crust with the mixture.

Bake the pie in a preheated 400° oven for 30 minutes, or until golden brown.

Remove from the oven to cool.

Serve the pie slightly warm with the strawberries in whipped cream alongside.

Yield: 8 to 10 servings

The Strawberries in Whipped Cream

Ingredients

1 cup heavy cream **1½ cups strawberries**

In the mixing bowl set with the whisk attachment, or with a hand beater, whip the heavy cream until stiff.

Wash and dry the strawberries and slice with a knife.

With a rubber spatula, fold the strawberries into the whipped cream.

Serve with the mince pie.

CRANBERRY GALETTE

(BLENDER OR STEEL BLADE; PASTRY OR WHISK ATTACHMENT)

This large, flat pie, perfect for Thanksgiving, is quite spectacular when filled with a glazed cranberry puree and decorated with swirls of candied orange rind. In principle, the galette is not all that different from the humble pizza: once the dough has risen, it is rolled in a circle, the edges folded in, then spread with the filling, and baked in a hot oven for a short time. Serve warm or at room temperature with a bowl of heavy cream, preferably unsweetened, beaten just until it holds its peaks.

The Dough

Ingredients

1 tablespoon dry active yeast
2 tablespoons butter
1 egg
1 tablespoon sugar

Pinch of salt
1 cup flour
Butter for the baking sheet

In a small bowl, dissolve yeast in ¼ cup of warm water.

In the work bowl, or in the mixing bowl set with the pastry or whisk attachment, place the butter, egg, sugar, and salt. Run the food processor for about 2 minutes.

Add the flour and the yeast, and run the food processor for another minute, or until the dough is elastic.

Flour a bowl and place the dough in it. Cover with a dish towel and set in a warm spot in your kitchen, or in a 200° oven, for 1½ hours, or until the dough rises.

The Cranberry Filling

Ingredients

1 15-ounce package of
  cranberries
1 cup orange juice
½ cup sugar

½ cup water
2 tablespoons cornstarch
2 tablespoons ice water
½ cup very fine sugar

Rinse the cranberries. Place in a saucepan with the orange juice, sugar, and water. Bring to a boil, lower the heat, and cook for 10 minutes, or until the cranberries have popped their skins.

Remove from heat and let cool for 10 minutes.

Pour the cranberries and the liquid into the blender or work bowl and run the food processor for 2 minutes, or until you have a fine puree.

Add the puree to a saucepan.

In a small bowl, mix the cornstarch with the ice water.

Stir the cornstarch into the cranberry puree and cook for a few minutes until the filling thickens slightly. Remove from the heat and let cool.

The Candied Orange Rind

Ingredients

Rind of ½ orange
½ cup water

½ cup sugar
½ teaspoon cognac

Slice the orange rind into very thin strips.

In a saucepan, bring the water, sugar, and cognac to a boil. Cook over a high heat until the syrup is reduced by half.

Add the orange rinds and boil in the syrup for about 10 minutes, until the rinds turn golden and begin to brown.

Using a slotted spoon, spread the candied rinds over a china plate to keep them from sticking together.

Assemble and bake the galette:

Form a ball with the dough. Then on a floured board, using a floured rolling pin, roll the dough into a circle 12 inches in diameter.

With your fingers, fold in the edges as you would for a pizza.

Butter the surface of a large baking sheet. Transfer the dough, by draping it over the rolling pin, onto the baking sheet.

Spread the cranberry puree over the pie shell.

Sprinkle ½ cup of very fine sugar over the puree.

Bake the galette in a preheated 450° oven for 15 minutes until the crust is golden.

Remove from the oven and decorate with a circle of swirls of orange rind chains. Roll a rind tightly and place in the center of the galette (see illustration).

Allow the galette to cool to room temperature.
Slice the galette at the table and serve with whipped cream.

Yield: 12 servings

RUM CREAM MOLD
(BLENDER OR STEEL OR PLASTIC BLADE; WHISK ATTACHMENT OR HAND
BEATER; SLICING BLADE; FOLDING ATTACHMENT, IF AVAILABLE)

Ingredients

1 envelope gelatin
4 egg yolks
⅔ cup sugar

¼ cup rum
2 cups heavy cream
2 squares semisweet chocolate

In the top of a double boiler or a small bowl, dissolve the gelatin in ½ cup of water. Place over simmering water and cook until all the gelatin has dissolved.

Place the yolks in the blender or work bowl and run the food processor for 20 seconds, or until the yolks are a pale yellow.

With the food processor running, add the sugar, a tablespoon at a time, through the feed tube.

Pour the gelatin through the feed tube and continue running the food processor for 4 seconds.

Add the rum and run for 2 more seconds. Transfer the egg mixture to a bowl.

In the mixing bowl set with the whisk attachment, or using a hand beater, beat the cream until it holds its shape.

With a rubber spatula, or the whisk or folding attachment, gently fold the beaten cream into the egg mixture.

Pour the mixture into a 1½-quart mold.

Chill in the refrigerator for 2 hours, or until the cream is firm.

Set the slicing blade in place. Fit the chocolate squares in the feed tube and push through to shave the chocolate.

To serve, unmold the rum cream dessert onto a small platter and sprinkle the shaved chocolate on top.

Yield: 6 servings

CLAFOUTI WITH PEACHES
(SLICING BLADE; BLENDER OR STEEL OR PLASTIC BLADE)

Ingredients

1½ pounds fresh, ripe peaches
3 tablespoons cognac
½ cup flour
½ cup plus 3 tablespoons sugar
3 eggs

Pinch of salt
1 cup milk
1 cup light cream
¼ cup confectioner's sugar
Butter for greasing the pan

Preheat the oven to 375°.

Drop the peaches in boiling water for about 10 seconds to loosen the skins. Peel the peaches and slice in half; remove the pits.

Set the slicing blade in place. Place a peach half upright in the feed tube and push through to slice. Repeat with each half until all are sliced.

Transfer the peaches to a bowl, pour the cognac over, and let stand for 1 hour, if possible, or while you make the batter.

In the blender or work bowl, place the flour, ½ cup of sugar, the eggs, and salt. Run the food processor for 5 seconds. Stop the machine and, if necessary, scrape the sides with a rubber spatula.

Now, with the food processor running, pour the milk and the cream at a moderate pace through the feed tube. Continue running the food processor until the mixture is the consistency of a pancake batter.

With a pat of butter, grease a shallow 1½-quart oven-to-table dish, such as a gratin pan.

Sprinkle 3 tablespoons of sugar over the bottom.

Spread the peaches over the bottom of the dish.

Pour the batter over the peaches.*

Place in a preheated 375° oven for 45 to 50 minutes until the custard is puffed and golden brown; it is done when a straw stuck in the center comes out clean.

Sprinkle with confectioner's sugar and serve warm.

Yield: 8 to 10 servings

* The clafouti can be prepared several hours in advance to this point.

STEAMED PERSIMMON PUDDING WITH BRANDY SAUCE
(BLENDER OR STEEL BLADE; WHISK ATTACHMENT OR HAND BEATER; FOLDING ATTACHMENT, IF AVAILABLE)

The Pudding

Ingredients

4 ripe persimmons
1 cup seedless raisins
2 tablespoons butter
1 cup milk
2 teaspoons brandy
2 cups sugar

4 teaspoons baking soda
2 cups all-purpose flour
½ teaspoon salt
1 cup almonds
Butter for the mold

Wash the persimmons and remove the stems, the skins, and the center pits.

Place the persimmon pulp in the blender or work bowl. Add the raisins and run the food processor for 15 seconds, or until pureed.

Meanwhile, in a small saucepan, melt the butter. Pour it into the persimmon puree.

Add the milk, brandy, and sugar, and run the food processor for 10 seconds.

Mix the baking soda, flour, and salt together in a bowl. Add to the blender or the work bowl. Run the food processor for 10 seconds, or until well mixed.

Butter a 1½-quart mold. Pour in the persimmon pudding and cover with aluminum foil.

Set in a pan of simmering water, halfway up the sides of the mold, and steam for 2 hours on top of the stove.

Meanwhile, blanch the almonds in boiling water for 5 seconds. Drain and remove the skins.

Place in the blender or work bowl and run the food processor until the almonds are chopped. Reserve.

Unmold the pudding when cooked. Serve warm, preferably, or at room temperature, covered with brandy sauce and sprinkled with chopped nuts.

The Brandy Sauce

Ingredients

4 egg yolks
2 cups very fine sugar

6–8 tablespoons brandy
1 pint heavy cream

An hour or more before serving time, place the egg yolks in the blender or work bowl and run the food processor for 5 seconds.

With the food processor running, pour the very fine sugar and the brandy through the feed tube. Continue running until well mixed.

In the mixing bowl set with the whisk attachment, or with a hand beater, beat the cream until it holds its peaks.

Using the whisk or folding attachment or a rubber spatula, fold the egg mixture into the cream.

Chill in a bowl in the refrigerator.

Just before serving, pour the brandy sauce over the pudding; sprinkle with the reserved chopped nuts. If you have used a very fine mold, serve the brandy sauce alongside in a sauceboat.

Yield: 8 servings

PUMPKIN MOUSSE WITH LEMON SAUCE
(BLENDER OR STEEL BLADE; WHISK ATTACHMENT OR HAND BEATER; FOLDING ATTACHMENT, IF AVAILABLE; SHREDDING BLADE)

The Mousse

Ingredients

2 envelopes unflavored gelatin
4 egg yolks
⅓ cup plus 2 tablespoons sugar
2 cups fresh or canned
   pumpkin puree
1 teaspoon cinnamon

1 teaspoon nutmeg
1 teaspoon allspice
Dash of ground cloves
1 tablespoon cognac
1 cup heavy cream

Place the gelatin and 4 tablespoons of water in the top of a double boiler or in a small bowl. Set over simmering water until the gelatin has dissolved completely.

Place the egg yolks and sugar in the blender or work bowl and run the food processor for 20 seconds, or until the yolks are a pale yellow.

With the food processor running, add the pumpkin puree through the feed tube.

Add the spices and the cognac.

Pour in the gelatin and continue running the food processor until the puree is mixed well. Remove the pumpkin mixture to a bowl.

[253]

In the mixing bowl, beat the cream until it holds its shape, using the whisk attachment or a hand beater.

With a rubber spatula, or the whisk or folding attachment, gently fold the cream into the pumpkin mixture.

Pour the pumpkin mousse into a 1½-quart mold and chill overnight in the refrigerator.

To serve, dip the mold quickly in hot water and unmold the mousse onto a platter. Serve the mousse with warm lemon sauce.

The Lemon Sauce

Ingredients

½ teaspoon grated lemon rind
⅓ cup sugar
1 tablespoon cornstarch
Pinch of salt

1 cup water
4 tablespoons butter
3½ teaspoons lemon juice

Set the shredding blade in place. Cut the lemon rind in several pieces, fit in the feed tube, and push through to grate; set aside.

In a saucepan, place the sugar, cornstarch, and salt. Slowly stir in the water.

Heat the mixture over a low heat, stirring all the while, until all the ingredients have dissolved and the liquid is fairly thick.

Remove the mixture from the heat. Add the butter, lemon juice, and grated lemon rind. Stir until the butter has melted and the sauce is mixed well.

Keep the sauce warm on the side of the stove until serving time. Serve in a sauceboat alongside the mousse.

Yield: 6 to 8 servings

BANANA MOUSSE PIE

Ingredients

Sweet pâte brisée (see
  page 41)
¼ pound almonds, shelled
  (optional)
6 ripe bananas
½ cup sugar

2 tablespoons rum or kirsch
4 egg whites
Pinch of salt
2 tablespoons very fine sugar
2 tablespoons confectioner's
  sugar

Preheat the oven to 375°.

Butter a 9-inch pie plate, preferably one with high, straight sides. Roll the dough on a floured board, fit it in the pie plate, and prick the bottom with a fork.

Bake the pie shell in a preheated 375° oven for 20 minutes, or until golden. Remove from the oven.

Meanwhile, toast the shelled almonds on a baking sheet in the oven for about 7 minutes, or until crisp; set aside.

Peel the bananas and place 4 in the blender or work bowl.

Add the granulated sugar and the rum or kirsch, and run the food proccesor for a minute, or until the bananas are a thick paste. Transfer to a bowl.

In the mixing bowl set with the whisk attachment or using a hand beater, beat the egg whites with a pinch of salt until quite stiff.

Using a rubber spatula, or the whisk or folding attachment, gently fold the egg whites into the banana mixture.

Pour the banana mousse into the pie shell.

Set the slicing blade in place. Fit the remaining 2 bananas in the feed tube and push through to slice.

Make a circle, with half the banana slices, around the edge of the pie.

About 25 minutes before dessert time, place the pie in a pre-heated 375° oven and bake for 20 minutes, or until the mousse is light and rises.

Remove the pie from the oven. Make another circle around the edge of the pie with the remaining banana slices.

Sprinkle the top with toasted almonds and dust with very fine sugar.

Set the pie under the broiler for a few seconds until the top is lightly toasted.

Dust with confectioner's sugar and serve at once.

Yield: 6 to 8 servings

RASPBERRY APPLE PIE
(WHISK ATTACHMENT OR STEEL BLADE; SLICING BLADE)

Raspberry and apple, an enticing blend of sweet and tart, make this deep-dish pie a favorite among dessert-lovers and non-dessert-lovers alike. Since fresh raspberries have a very short season, we often make this with frozen, unsweetened berries, with excellent results.

Ingredients

Sweet pâte brisée for the top
  crust (see page 41)
3 pints raspberries, fresh or
  frozen
1 pound cooking apples, or
  3 medium MacIntosh apples

2 tablespoons butter
½ cup plus 3 tablespoons
  sugar
1 tablespoon very fine sugar

Preheat the oven to 425°.

Prepare the sweet pâte brisée and refrigerate for 1 hour.

If the raspberries are frozen, let thaw and drain. If fresh, rinse in cold water and drain well.

Peel, core, and quarter the apples.

Set the slicing blade in place, fit the apples in the feed tube, and push through to slice.

In a skillet, melt the butter. When it is hot, add the apples and ½ cup of sugar. Turn the heat low and cook for several minutes until the apples are tender but not falling apart. Remove from the heat and let cool for 10 minutes.

In the bottom of a baking dish, preferably one used for making deep-dish pies, pack the berries.

Sprinkle 3 tablespoons of sugar over them.

Spread the apples evenly on top.

Retrieve the pâte brisée from the refrigerator. On a floured board, using a floured rolling pin, roll the dough into a circle.

Drape the dough over the apples and, with your fingers, roll any excess dough back inside the baking dish and press it up and along the inside edge to form a rim.

In the center of the dough, make a cross with a knife blade. Fold each of the triangles back so that a small window opens in the center.

Brush the crust with cold water and sprinkle with 1 tablespoon of very fine sugar.

Bake in a preheated 425° oven for 25 minutes, or until the crust is golden brown.

Serve at once, accompanied by heavy cream, whipped cream, or vanilla ice cream.

Yield: 6 servings

CHOCOLATE TRUFFLES
(BLENDER OR STEEL BLADE)

These rich candies, heady with brandy, need no cooking and call for ingredients you may already have on hand. Unfortunately, whether you make them for a party or for your own enjoyment, they must stand in the refrigerator for a day or two.

Ingredients

2 teaspoons unsweetened cocoa

2 tablespoons brandy

½ cup whole walnuts, almonds, pecans, or hazelnuts, shelled

4 tablespoons butter, cut in small pieces

2 cups confectioner's sugar

2 tablespoons corn syrup

1 tablespoon heavy cream

Pinch of salt

Extra cocoa

In the blender or work bowl, place the cocoa, brandy, ¼ cup of nuts, butter cut in small pieces, confectioner's sugar, corn syrup, heavy cream, and a pinch of salt. Run the food processor for 1½ minutes, stopping the motor once or twice to scrape the sides with a rubber spatula.

Continue running the food processor until the mixture is a thick paste. Remove to a bowl.

Roll the cocoa mixture, between the palms of your hands, into small balls about 1 inch in diameter.

Place the remaining ¼ cup of nuts in the blender or work bowl. Run the food processor for 35 seconds, or until chopped fine.

Pour the chopped nuts into a small dish. Pour the extra cocoa into another.

Roll half the balls first in the chopped nuts, then in the extra cocoa.

Roll the other half in the extra cocoa first, then in the chopped nuts.

Place in a sealed container or in aluminum foil and chill in the refrigerator for 24 hours.

Yield: About 30 candies

WALNUT PUFFS
(BLENDER OR STEEL BLADE; WHISK ATTACHMENT OR HAND BEATER; FOLDING ATTACHMENT, IF AVAILABLE)

Ingredients

1½ cups walnuts, shelled
1 tablespoon flour
½ cup brown sugar

4 egg whites
Pinch of salt
Oil for cookie sheet

Preheat the oven to 300°.

Place 1 cup of walnuts in the blender or work bowl. Run the food processor for 25 seconds, or until very finely grated. Remove to a medium bowl.

Add the remaining ½ cup of walnuts and run the food processor until coarsely chopped, about 10 seconds. Add to the bowl.

Pour the flour and brown sugar into the bowl with the walnuts and mix well.

Place the egg whites in the mixing bowl set with the whisk attachment, or use a hand beater. Add a pinch of salt to the egg whites and beat until very stiff.

Using a rubber spatula, or the whisk or folding attachment, gently fold the walnut mixture into the egg whites.

Line a cookie sheet with waxed paper and grease lightly with oil.

Using a teaspoon, drop the batter onto the oiled waxed paper.

Place in a preheated 300° oven and bake for 20 minutes, or until lightly brown and slightly resilient to the touch.

Using a spatula, remove the cookies to a platter to cool and harden slightly before serving.

Yield: About 25 cookies

THIN BUTTER COOKIES
(WHISK ATTACHMENT OR STEEL OR PLASTIC BLADE)

Ingredients

1 stick butter, cut in small pieces
½ cup sugar
1 egg, separated

Pinch of salt
1 cup flour
2 tablespoons cinnamon
½ cup very fine sugar

Preheat the oven to 350°.

In the mixing bowl set with the whisk attachment or in the work bowl, place the butter cut in small pieces and the sugar. Run the food processor for 10 seconds, or until the mixture is light and fluffy.

With the food processor running, add the egg yolk and salt.

Gradually add the flour and continue running the food processor for 3 seconds more.

Remove the dough and gather it together. Separate and roll into balls the size of marbles.

Grease a cookie sheet and lightly flour the bottom of a shot glass.

Place the balls of dough on the cookie sheet and press down on them with the shot glass to form thin rounds.

With a fork, beat the egg white lightly. Brush the surface of each cookie with the egg white.

In a bowl, mix the cinnamon and very fine sugar together. Sprinkle the cinnamon-sugar over the cookies.

Bake in a preheated 350° oven for 8 to 10 minutes. When the cookies are golden brown, turn off the oven and let cool.

Yield: 30 cookies

BROWNIES
(WHISK ATTACHMENT OR PLASTIC BLADE)

Ingredients

4 eggs

4 ounces unsweetened chocolate

2 cups sugar

1 stick butter, cut in small pieces

1 cup flour

2 teaspoons vanilla

1 teaspoon salt

¾ cup raisins soaked in 2 tablespoons brandy for an hour (optional)

Confectioner's sugar

Preheat the oven to 325°.

In the mixing bowl set with the whisk attachment or in the work bowl, place the eggs and beat for 10 seconds. Remove to a bowl.

Melt the chocolate and sugar together in the top of a double boiler or in a saucepan over low heat, stirring all the while with a wooden spoon.

Place the butter in the mixing bowl or work bowl, and run the food processor for about 15 seconds, or until the butter is creamed.

Add the chocolate and sugar and run the food processor until mixed well.

With the food processor running, pour in the beaten eggs and mix for 5 seconds.

Add the flour, vanilla, and salt and run the food processor for 15 seconds, or until well blended.

Add the raisins to the batter and run the food processor for a fraction of a second to mix.

Pour the batter into 2 buttered 8-inch-square pans.

Bake in a preheated 325° oven for 20 to 30 minutes.

Remove the brownies from the oven and let cool for 15 minutes before cutting into squares.

Sprinkle with confectioner's sugar and serve.

Yield: About 30 brownies

TUILES
(SLICING BLADE; WHISK ATTACHMENT OR PLASTIC BLADE)

These very delicate cookies are splendid with ice cream or with berries in cream. To achieve their traditional, slightly curved shape, set the tuiles, fresh from the oven, astride a rolling pin to harden; then pile them, one on top of another, and serve.

Ingredients

¼ pound shelled almonds, or ½ cup toasted and slivered almonds	4 drops vanilla
	⅓ cup flour
	½ cup sugar
4 tablespoons butter	Butter for cookie sheet
2 egg whites	

Preheat the oven to 325°.

Blanch the almonds in boiling water for 5 to 6 seconds. Drain and remove the skins.

Set the slicing blade in place. Pack the feed tube with the almonds and push through to sliver.

Spread the almonds on a baking sheet and toast in a preheated 325° oven for 5 or 6 minutes, or until golden brown. Remove the almonds to a bowl.

Raise the oven heat to 400°.

Melt the butter.

In the mixing bowl set with the whisk attachment, or in the work bowl set with the plastic blade, place the egg whites and vanilla. Run the food processor for 2½ seconds until the whites are light and fluffy.

Add the flour, butter, sugar, and almonds. Run the food processor until all the ingredients are well mixed, about 4 minutes.

Butter a cookie sheet and drop the batter by half-teaspoons onto the sheet, leaving 2 inches between each cookie.

Bake in a preheated 400° oven for 7 or 8 minutes, or until lightly browned.

While still hot, remove the cookies, one by one, with a spatula and lay astride a rolling pin to harden into slightly curved, or convex, cookies.

Place any cookies that harden before they have been shaped back in the oven for a minute or two to soften them.

Place the cookies on a platter, stack if you wish, and serve.

Yield: 30 cookies

Index

Mornay sauce, 183–184
with paprika, 187
Beef
brisket of beef with cranberries and green peppercorns, 115–117
brisket or pot roast
Parisian pastry sticks, 225–226
potatoes stuffed with, 229
chick pea fritters, 224-225
filet mignon stuffed with marrow, 119–121
dough for wrapping filet of, 31
fondue Bourguignonne, 122–125
condiments and sauces, 123–125
dill mustard sauce, 125
fondue, 122
hot Haitian sauce, 124
mayonnaise Aïoli, 123–124
ground
hamburgers, 125–126
steak au poivre, 125–126
marinade for, 115
Parmentier (with potatoes and peas), 220–221
paupiettes of beef with Foyot sauce, 117–119
stock, 86–87
jus lié (quick brown sauce), 191
stuffed cabbage with, 230–231

stuffed vine leaves, 223–224
Beets
cold cucumber and beet soup, 103
cranberry beet soup, 109–110
endive and beet salad, 74–75
beurre manié, 132
making in blender, xiv
mixing with steel blade, xii
Bird's-Nest Maker, 202–204
for straw potato baskets, 202–204
Black olive soup, 107–108
Blenders
grating bread crumbs, xiv
meat and fish ground in, xiv
See also Food Processors
Bluefish en croûte, 159–160
Bosch Magic Mixer, Deluxe, 1, 2–5
Blue cheese
butter seasoned with, 79
accessories, 3–5
Brandy sauce, 252–253
Braun Kitchen Machine, 1, 5–7
accessories, 5–7
Breads
croutons, 91, 111–112
Bread crumbs
grating, 25
grating in blender, xiv
processed in quantity, xi, xiv
Bretonne sauce, 186
Broccoli
cream of broccoli soup, 91–92

Butter cookies, 260–261
Butters, 79–81
  herbal, 80–81
  marrow, 79–80
  seasoned with Blue Cheese, 79
  seasoned with horseradish, 81
  tarragon, 121

C

Cabbage
  sauté with bacon and wine, 145
  shredding, 145
  stuffed, 230–231
Cakes
  deep chocolate cake with hazelnuts, 239–241
  gateau of crepes filled with apricot soufflé, 241–243
  Reston Virginia bourbon cake, 237–238
Capers
  lemon caper sauce, 193
Carrots
  and leek soup, 93
  chopping or slicing, xiii, 150
Casserole dishes
  lamb ragout, 154–155
  Parmentier, 220–221
Cauliflower
  puree of, 209–210
  raw cauliflower salad, 213
  slicing, 213

Celery
  cold celery and potato soup, 105
  grandmother's soup, 97–98
  Rémoulade, 75–76
Cheese
  blue
    butter seasoned with, 79
    fried potato puffs with, 206–207
  grating, 25 88
    processing in quantity, xi, xiv
  and ham soufflé, 52-54
  Mornay sauce, 183–184
  Parmesan
    grating, xi
    pesto sauce, 187–188
  Roquefort dressing, 196
  slicing, 88
  sticks, 45
Chick pea fritters, 224–225
Chicken
  browning, 142–143
  chick pea fritters, 224–225
  cold chicken en croûte, 217–218
  cold chicken farci Edith Ferber, 138–139
  curry Tabinta, 146–147
  deboning, 139–140
  four-meat pâté, 58–63
  mock chicken quenelles with lemon sauce, 218–220
  stock, 85–86
  stuffed cabbage with, 230–231

Cream puffs
   Pâte à choux or puff pastry
      dough, 45–46
   See also Puff shells
Crepes
   assembling and baking, 165
   batter, 35–36
      for lobster soufflé, 163
   cooking, 36, 163
   gateau of crepes filled with
      apricot soufflé, 241–243
   hors d'oeuvres, 35–37
      with smoked salmon, 36–
         37
      stuffed with mushrooms,
         37–38
Croutons, 91, 111–112
Crudités, or raw vegetables, 78
   seasoned butters, 74–81
Cucumbers
   cold cucumber and beet soup,
      103
   gazpacho, 110–112
   salad with yogurt, 77–78
   and string bean soup, 102
   trout with cucumber stuffing,
      158–159
Cuisinart Food Processor, 1, 8–
      10
   accessories, 8–10
   grating hard cheeses, xi
Curry dishes
   curry Tabinta, 146–147
   Indonesian chicken curry, 146
   puff shells with crabmeat and
      lemon caper sauce, 49–50

D

Deep-frying
   chick pea fritters, 224-225
   julienne potatoes, 203
   potato puffs with cheese, 206–
      207
Desserts, 236–263
   banana mousse pie, 255–256
   brownies, 261
   chocolate truffles, 258–259
   clafouti with peaches, 250–
      251
   cranberry galette, 246–249
      candied orange rind, 247–
         249
      cranberry filling, 247
      dough, 246
   cream puffs, 45
   deep chocolate cake with ha-
      zelnuts, 239–241
   eclairs, 45
   gateau of crepes filled with
      apricot soufflé, 241–243
   gelatin
      pumpkin mousse with
         lemon sauce, 253–254
      rum cream mold, 249–250
   mince pie served with straw-
      berries in whipped
      cream, 243–245
   pumpkin mousse with lemon
      sauce, 253–254
   raspberry apple pie, 256–257
   Reston Virginia bourbon
      cake, 237–138

[269]

G

Game birds
  stuffed game hens on bed of
    cabbage, 144–146
Garlic
  Aïoli mayonnaise, 123–124,
    181
  black olive soup, 107–108
  soup with almonds, 98–99
  vinaigrette dressing, 195
Gazpacho, 110–112
  garnish ingredients, 110–111
Ginger, shredding fresh, 204
Grandmother's soup, 97–98
Gratinéed dishes
  Mornay sauce, 183–184
  onion soup gratinée
  puree of cauliflower, 209–210
  sauce supreme, 185
Green mayonnaise, 179–180
Green peppercorns
  brisket of beef with cranber-
    ries and, 115–117

H

Haitian sauce, 124
Halibut soufflé, 50
Ham
  and cheese soufflé, 52–54
  mousse with morels in aspic,
    67–69
  stuffed eggs à la coque, 221–
    222

Hazelnuts
  blanching and skinning, 239
  chocolate cake with, 239–241
    chocolate icing, 241
Herbs
  fines herbes sauce, 192
  pastry, 150
  quiche with tomatoes, ancho-
    vies, and herbs, 43–44
  seasoned butters, 80–81
  vinaigrette dressing, 196
Holiday turkey pie, 227–228
Hollandaise sauce, 173–174
  Béarnaise sauce, 174
  making ahead of time, 174
  Mousseline sauce, 175–176
Hors d'oeuvres, 29–81
  cheese sticks, 45
  cold, 57–81
    bay scallop salad, 71–72
    crudités or raw vegetables,
      78
    seasoned butters, 79–81
    duck pâté, 62–64
    four-meat pâté, 57–61
    ham mousse with morels in
      aspic, 67–69
    pâtés, 57–64
    Rillettes, 64–65
    seasoned butters, 79–81
      butter seasoned with
        blue cheese, 79
      butter with horseradish,
        81
      herbal butter, 80–81
      marrow butter, 79–80

[274]

I

J

Julienne potatoes, 202
    baskets with peas, 202–204
    preparing, xiii
Jus lié (quick brown sauce),
    191
    sauce piquante, 194

K

Kitchen Aid Model K5-A, 1, 13–
    16
    accessories, 3–16

L

Lamb
    chick pea fritters, 224–225
    Parmentier (with potatoes
        and peas), 220–221
    ragout, 154–155
    stuffed cabbage with, 230–231
    stuffed leg of lamb in herb
        pastry, 149–154
        herb pastry, 150
        leg of lamb, 150–153
        roasting, 152–154
        wrapping in pastry, 152–
        153
    stuffed vine leaves, 223–224
Leeks
    carrot and leek soup, 93
    grandmother's soup, 97–98
    and hard-boiled egg salad, 214
Leftovers, 216–234
    chick pea fritters, 224–225

cold chicken en croûte, 217–
    218
fish croquettes with Fumet
    sauce, 231–233
fish or shellfish salad, 233–
    234
holiday turkey pie, 227–229
mock chicken quenelles with
    lemon sauce, 218–220
Parisian pastry sticks, 225–226
Parmentier, 220-221
stuffed cabbage, 230–231
stuffed eggs à la coque, 221–
    222
stuffed potatoes, 229
stuffed vine leaves, 223–224
Lemon caper sauce, 193
Lemon sauce
    for escarole, 205–206
    mock chicken quenelles, 218–
    220
    for pumpkin mousse, 254
Lobster
    soufflé in crepes with Coulis
        sauce, 162–163
    Coulis sauce, 166
    crepes, 163
    soufflé, 164–165

M

Marinades
    yogurt for chicken, 146
Marrow
    butter, 79–80

puff pastry (pâte à choux) dough, 45–46
  with sweetbreads and sauce piquante, 47
Pumpkin mousse with lemon sauce, 253–254
Purees
  artichoke, 207–208
  cauliflower, 209–210
  cranberries, 247
  sorrel, 208–209

Q

Quenelles
  mock chicken quenelles with lemon sauce, 218–220
Quiche
  Baking shell, 41
  Lorraine with onions and bacon, 42
  pâte brisée for shell, 41
  with tomatoes, anchovies and herbs, 43–44

R

Raspberry apple pie, 256–257
Raspberry soup, 108–109
Rice
  apricot filling for crown roast of pork, 133–135
  scallop of veal with vegetables, 128–130
  stuffed vine leaves, 223
Rillettes, 64–65
  mixed spices for, 30

Robot Coupe Model R-a, 1, 19–21
  accessories, 19–21
  egg-based sauces, xii
  grating hard cheeses, xi
Rock cornish game hens
  stuffed game hens on bed of cabbage, 144–146
Romaine and marrow soup, 95
Roquefort dressing, 196
Roux, 182, 183
Rum cream mold, 249–250

S

Saffron
  chicken curry Tabinta, 146–147
  preparation, 147
Salad dressings and vinaigrettes, 195–198
  for celery Rémoulade, 75–76
  chiffonade dressing, 197
  classic vinaigrette, 195
  garlic vinaigrette, 195
  herbal vinaigrette, 196
  Roquefort dressing, 196
  vinaigrette Normandy, 198
Salads
  avocado, 70
  celery Rémoulade, 75–76
  cucumber with yogurt, 77–78
  endive and beet salad, 74–75
  fish or shellfish, 233–234
  hot potato salad, 210–211
  leek and hard-boiled egg salad, 214

[283]

Tarragon
  Béarnaise sauce, 174–175
  butter, 121
  herbe pastry, 150
Tarte aux moules (mussels),
    156–158
Tarts and tartlets, dough for, 31
Tomatoes
  Choron sauce, 175
  cold tomato and basil soup,
    101–102
  fresh tomato puree, 44
  gazpacho, 110–112
  hot Haitian sauce, 124
  quiche with tomatoes, ancho-
    vies and herbs, 43
  sauces, 175, 188–189
Trout
  with cucumber stuffing, 158–
    159
Tuiles (almond cookies), 262–
    263
Turkey
  chick pea fritters,, 224–225
  holiday turkey pie, 227–228
    dough, 227
    turkey filling, 228

V
Veal
  chops passetto, 127–128
  mousse with paprika sauce,
    131–132
  scallop of veal with vegeta-
    bles, 128–130
Vegetable slicer/shredders, xv

Vegetables
  artichoke puree, 207–208
  beans
    cucumber and string bean
      soup, 102
    lamb or beef cooked with
      potatoes and, 220–221
  beets
    cold cucumbers and beet
      soup, 103
    cranberry beet soup, 109–
      110
  broccoli
    cream of broccoli soup, 91–
      92
  cabbage
    sautéed with bacon and
      wine, 145
    stuffed, 230–231
  carrots
    carrot and leek soup, 93
    scallop of veal with vegeta-
      bles, 128–130
  cauliflower
    puree of, 209–210
    raw cauliflower salad, 213
  celery
    cold celery and potato
      soup, 105–106
    grandmother's soup, 97–98
  chick pea fritters, 224–225
  crudités, 78
    seasoned butters, 79–81
      blue cheese, 79
      herbal butter, 80–81
      marrow butter, 79–80